Love

TAMARA PLANT

ISBN: 1987722620
ISBN-13: 978-1987722628

Dedication

Love is dedicated to the souls who have
passed through my life to teach me these lessons,
and to those who need to learn them.

Acknowledgements

Special thanks to **Molly McCord** for guiding me to
write this book, and talking me off the ledge
at the very last second.

To Bernice, Karissa, Teresa, Karen, Sue, and Sheena,
thank you for allowing me to have these
conversations with soulmates.

To everyone who followed my writing journey on social
media (especially my badass Instagram followers),
thank you for sticking with me.
I hope *Love* lives up to your expectations.

Foreword

As a kid, I always found myself rooting for the underdog. As I grew up, I realized there is much to be said for the underdogs of the world; the ones who find a way to rise despite their struggles and limitations. I cheered for the worst teams and wanted to learn about people who came from tough places. I thought the comeback was heroic and inspirational. I didn't realize the journey they went through to get to the place that could break you. I learned the hard way as a teen, when I was picked up and flung headfirst into Underdogdom.

What I'd imagined as a motivational turning point turned out to be a brutal disappointment to the reality I experienced. But I'll get to that in a second.

The black misery of that place helped me quickly recognize a light when it flickered in the distance. And one day, that light lit the path for me to the soul of a woman named Tamara Plant. I can't even remember how it all started, but I found myself nominated for the Rising Star award through her FIERCE Women of the Year event in

2011. Chatting back and forth with her and then meeting her for the first time, I was captivated by her presence. THIS woman was fierce. She lit fires and stirred shit up. I loved her honesty, her truth, and her edge. She was a fucking badass with a story, and I was gonna absorb that energy every chance I could. I needed the boost.

Early on I learned life can be such a bitch. She's a manipulative, tricky, evil bitch.

Sometimes.

Other times she's warm and comfortable, and fun but that's where the manipulation comes in. I've laughed with life until I peed myself (so have you), I've screamed at it in anguish, and I've felt every single sensation in between.

Two months before I turned 16, a train hit my Mom's car, and she was gone. In my relatively comfortable and sheltered existence before December 1st, 1997, I never could have fathomed the heartbreak and pain of a loss of this magnitude.

The physical stress of a traumatic separation is overwhelming.

There were nights where I didn't think I would be able to calm my racing heart or catch my breath; I was violently hyperventilating and sobbing. The panic and stress of suddenly having your world ripped out from under you was the most intense and debilitating feeling I'd ever experienced. My security was gone. Suddenly I didn't know who I was or what I could ever become. My family had only just moved 9 hours from the town we grew up in the year before, so after Mom passed, we ended up moving again for Dad's work. I was in three different schools in five years, so I didn't get attached to anyone (aside from the boyfriend I was dragging through it all like a security blanket).

For ten years my family of four - my Dad, younger sister and brother, and me - struggled to move forward. We all went through the motions of daily life, but every single day we felt the bitterness of loss that permeated everything we did. If Mom were here, *this* would be different. I could be better at *that* if I had a Mom supporting me.

I lived in a gray space, numb to every emotion. It was suddenly clear to me: THIS was how people became angry and miserable. Life takes a jab at you every now and again, and sometimes you lose everything. You're a loser now, I told myself. If you had a Mom, you would be out meeting people and having fun instead of crying at the drop of a hat and bringing everyone down around you.

Good luck with life, I thought.

What kind of Mother could you ever be? How will you hold a job? How will anyone love you through all this? I just knew this life is going to be a long and miserable one.

Perhaps it was divine intervention, but after a few years, I started to HEAR what I was telling myself. "Are you seriously listening to this crap?" I heard my mom say to me.

My anger, I decided, wasn't helping, and I made a conscious choice to be gentler and kinder to myself. What's it going to take to feel GOOD instead of miserable, I wondered? OK, let's find one good thing that happened today. Huh, that wasn't so difficult, I thought.

Some days were easier than others, and on the tough days, I gave myself space to be upset.

On the good days, I let myself *feel* good without any guilt, and when I was stuck in my head, I concentrated intensely to accomplish that. I didn't do anything for fun, and I didn't have a lot of friends. I worked at a job I hated, with people I didn't relate to and sat around waiting for my boyfriend to get home from working away, month after month after month. I was incredibly lonely.

I tried to be mad at other people, but they didn't react the way I needed them to respond; they didn't see the sadness masked by anger. Call me a quick learner, but it became apparent that changing ME would be easier than changing them. At first, this made me even more resentful, but it also made me start to choose myself over anyone else.

I asked myself what felt good? What did I want to do in that moment? I started doing little things, like cranking up the music as I cleaned the house. That felt amazing. I started opening windows and feeling the fresh air. That got me outside into the yard or walking trails. I started turning my face to the sun and stopping to feel its warmth, imaging the way it used to feel when Mom kissed my face. I began looking inward to find a new best friend, and with that, I started to receive Mom's messages more clearly.

As I went about my day working hard to be better, she laughed with me, cried with me, and we talked all the time. I started seeing what she would have wanted for me, and the path to get there became clear.

Once I got the hang of catching myself in my negativity, transformation became easier. The release was powerful and I began putting myself first. I started going to the gym. I quit my office job and applied for a serving position at an upscale lounge where I knew no one, forcing myself entirely out of my comfort zone. I grasped the basics of that job faster than I expected, and it was there that I got the chance to learn about myself in a new environment. I learned that I'm kinda fun to be around, and discovered I love to meet new people, and I thrive under pressure. Making money, being independent, and having a more responsibility than I was used to made me feel incredible.

From there, I focused on positive thinking

and finding the good in challenging situations. I began to read about enlightenment and purpose, and my perception changed completely. I moved away, back to where I considered close to "home," and my sister and I started a business. That junior high school sweetheart came with me, and we bought a house. We made plans, we accomplished goals, and along the way, I started to understand why I had to experience death the way I did.

Fast forward through a few years of having Tamara in my life since that divine connection at the awards. We've shared a lot of laughs and few tears (most of those tears were mine and most occurred through reading her first book, *Forgiveness & Other Stupid Things*). I was honoured when the invitation from this incredible woman came, asking me to write the foreword for her second book, *Love*. Tamara and I share many experiences with grief, loss, resilience, and transformation. She has shared so much with me over the years, and now she shares with you the cold hard truths behind the Ying and Yang of death, love, and soulmates.

She shows us why you can't fully experience love without risking something, and sometimes, risking a lot. We see that our personal growth is directly related to our experiences with vulnerability and that every single connection that we are blessed to have in our lives is unique and vital. We have much to learn from every experience we face, and when you are open enough to receive those lessons, your growth from it will be monumental.

I spent a long time creating habits and holding myself accountable for my happiness, even though I wasn't entirely sure that's what I was doing at the time. Once I started to give credit to my feelings while taking responsibility for my happiness, life began revealing people to me who validated this energy exchange and helped me see how relevant those habits were to my development and journey through grief.

Now, with powerful women like Tamara in my life sharing insight and wisdom from their own experiences, I am finally able to cherish that hazy space behind me where life hurt the most and felt the heaviest. I still cry when I think about what I lost when my mom died, but I embrace with enormous gratitude where it leads me.

With her feisty wit and energized emotion, Tamara will have you laughing and crying while turning every addicting page. You'll reflect on your journey with renewed optimism and strength and trust, knowing that with hurt comes openness and a chance to shed a layer to reveal a version of yourself you have GOT to meet.

You wait. She's gorgeous.

You're gonna love her.

Sheena Johnson, Owner of The Bra Lounge

Prologue

"Hey, what's up?"

"She committed suicide."

"What? What did you say?"

Death doesn't fuck around.

Birth is the beginning and death is the end, but it's the snapshots in between that create a life. These are monumental moments that we remember as twists of fate pushing us onto a detour we would never have taken if they didn't force us there. Sometimes they're tragic, other times they're beautiful and regardless of how they occurred, they stay with us forever.

Life is made of moments like that.

It's easy to figure out why I had to regenerate into new versions of myself over and over again. My life had been like some bizarre checklist:

- ✓ Abusive stepdad
- ✓ Alcoholic mom on welfare
- ✓ Homeless as a teenager
- ✓ Thoughts of suicide
- ✓ Death after death after death

Each moment blanketed layer upon layer of anger and hatred that eventually became so heavy; it almost buried me alive. I can look back and see the timeline of my life, pinpointing where I was at a crossroads, where chance encounters changed the direction I was going, and the detours that probably saved me from myself.

Looking back is easy.

When you understand why death is a part this journey, you begin to live life on purpose. You learn to bob and weave around the punches you think are coming as punishment from the universe in some twisted form of karma but the reality is that it's your choices that get you to critical junctures in your life. It doesn't mean you should wallow in blame or berate yourself for making stupid mistakes; it simply means that we're on a path that can be fraught with landmines. When you reach one, it propels you into another realm of awakening and ascension.

These landmines are always in the form of huge life moments caused by love, death, and soulmates that require leaps of faith, saying 'Fuck you' to fear and break you wide open exposing you to a pain you never thought possible.

Love: a heart-centric emotion for another person

Death: the physical end of the human experience

Soulmate: an energetic connection that transcends lifetime after lifetime

Tracking where you've been and how you got to where you are, helps to make sense out of the situations, you find yourself in but how do you know whether to go left, right, turn around or stand still? How do you come to an understanding of peace for yourself without completely sabotaging everything good in your life? You can't stay stuck in those moments otherwise you never move forward to create better ones so you must embrace every feeling, good or bad, and release it to move forward.

I had to learn that the hard way and I hope whatever I've overcome will be of some value to you so that you don't have to suffer alone.

Here's what I know: You're given a roadmap before you enter this lifetime, and once you learn to see the signs, the detours get shorter, and the path becomes wide open with possibilities.

The first step in exchanging pain for purpose is listening to the messages you need to hear. The thing about healing is that you can't do it until you're ready; only then will the wisdom become the light at the end of the tunnel that you've been searching for.

It doesn't matter if the messenger is in the form of song lyrics, movie quotes, billboards or fortune cookies; you'll recognize the message when it smacks you across the head. That's how I found Eminem. It wasn't like finding Jesus or some AHA moment, it was more of a, "Wow, I can relate to your pain and your resilience inspires me," kinda thing. I was given a copy of his *Recovery* album in 2010 and listened over and over to the songs, connecting to the messages of becoming the worst version of yourself to reclaiming your power by owning your story. Tracks like *Talkin' 2 Myself*, *Not Afraid*, and *Going Through Changes*, reached me on a spiritual level that Wayne Dyer couldn't at the time. I looked for more songs and found *'Till I Collapse*, *Lose Yourself*, *Survival*, *Lighters*, *Kings Never Die*, *Phenomenal* and his love letter of forgiveness to his mom, *Headlights*.

In *8 Mile*, Eminem's silver screen debut, one of the final scenes shows him owning his faults and circumstances during an epic rap battle by turning the spotlight on himself. It wasn't until years later when I discovered the art of self-awareness that the scene hit me on yet another spiritual level. I learned that by being OK with who I was despite the shit I had to go through to get to this place of inner peace, nothing anyone said about me would hold any power over me because I knew where I had fucked up and where I had made stupid decisions. I had also learned to forgive myself for the choices I had made along the way.

Once I was open to messages of healing and forgiving, it was easier to take a look at more woo-woo, hippy-dippy spiritual teachings like Wayne Dyer's work and go a little deeper into my recovery process. I began to intentionally listen to the messages that I needed regardless of the messenger and start, what I hoped was, the final transformation on this journey.

Death, however, had another plan.

So here we are.

You never know when you'll take your last breath or when you'll have that final conversation with someone or where you'll be when it happens. I've lost a lot of people in my 42 years on this earth: friends, family, coworkers, and mentors. If I made a list of the people I can remember who have died, it would add up to 30 something.

That's about one death every year and a half that I've been alive.

That's a lot of fucking death.

Their names won't mean anything to you, but their lives have all had some impact, some ripple effect on the world even if it's in the smallest way, they were here for a reason. With each death, I experienced change whether I realized it or not but what I know for sure is that there is no death without love or soulmate connections.

With each death, I felt a part of my soul break into pieces that I was sure would never mend. I became a shattered mosaic of the lives who'd touched mine, imperfectly fused together by emotional scar tissue like stained glass, telling a story of who they were and who I had become. I am the composite of every person I've lost on this journey however death doesn't mean the end of who they were for I continue, carrying a piece of them with me.

It's easy to be philosophical about death when you're not in the middle of grieving. It's easy to offer advice or defer to the "everything happens for a reason" or "their journey has ended" mentality when the death doesn't immediately impact you. But when you're crushed by grief and can't go on, nothing anyone says will make you feel better. You start searching for meaning and try to understand the why of it all, but healing is a personal journey that forces you to go within and discover your beliefs.

There is a moment between learning about the death of a loved one and when the reality of their death sets in, where you're suspended in time. Everything around you stops.

It's like being in a crowded room; the noise grinds to deafening silence and the people around you are frozen in time. The clock doesn't stop ticking, and although your body goes through the motions, a dense fog traps your mind refusing to let you escape. Death consumes you, the weight of grief envelops you, and the only way out is to keep moving even though you want to lay down and let it swallow you whole.

You might learn lessons that you didn't want to learn or resent the people around you for trying to help. Or you might be so angry that you had to go through it, but when you can get to a place of gratitude, you'll no longer fear the unknown and come to understand that the fog, like death, is merely an illusion.

It's tough to have any gratitude when someone dies. You feel robbed of time with that person; you'll never get to have a conversation with them or hug them or argue with them again. They've been ripped out of your life so why the fuck would gratitude ever enter the picture when all you feel is immeasurable emotional and physical pain? You're not grateful they've died; you learn to be grateful for the moments you had with them while they were here.

Death wakes you the fuck up to realize that other people around you will die, too, so you better stop taking them for granted and appreciate the moments you have with them while they're here.

Yeah, I get it.

It's easy to be reflective and thoughtful about death after you've healed from a loss but when you're going through it, the process is ugly and messy and finding comfort is nearly impossible.

Each death I've experienced has become a stepping stone to my spiritual understanding of what it all means. Sitting with grief and meditating has been one of the tools I've used to process death.

I want to be completely transparent before we go any further. I'm not religious in the traditional sense. I don't go to church, and I don't study or practice religion although I was raised in a Catholic environment and was even an altar girl when I was a teenager. I also studied Islam for a year when I was eight years old and lived in Kuwait with my grandparents. I've looked into other religions like Buddhism and Hinduism, adopting beliefs that speak to me on a soul level. They gave me something to believe in when I questioned everything I had been taught and stopped believing in anything at all. I've incorporated various pieces of multiple faiths into my life like some colourful patchwork of ideology. I'm particularly fond of Lord Ganesha, the Hindu God who looks like an elephant and is known for obliviating obstacles and providing abundance. I'm also cool with my Worry Buddha who takes away any anxiety or fear. I feel the energy transfer into the wooden sculpture which sits in the palm of my hand, and the release is like a full body sigh.

Most of all, I like to hang with the angels. A few years ago, I discovered Archangel Michael and his merry band of celestial muses after stumbling onto angel oracle cards and learning that angels are non-denominational. I'm down with that even though I give props to the Big G/Source/ Universe / whatever you want to call the divine spirit that chills within you. As for Archangel Michael, I've come to know him as a spiritual bodyguard. He's the Kevin Costner to my Whitney Houston, and The Rock to my Kevin Hart and the Deadpool to my Weasel. (sidenote, Deadpool is my spirit animal).

When I meditate and call upon Archangel Michael, it's like having a conversation with an old friend. I see him smiling as he comes down from the stars, sword secured on his back and wings as glorious as you could imagine. As he nears, we fist bump and nod at each other, like the spiritual badasses we are. I greet him with a "What's up," or "Hey," which is more of a statement than a question, and he smirks every single time.

Depending on the topic, we can be more somber or light-hearted in our conversations and I leave feeling better about the situation because I know he's got my back. Archangel Michael is the only angel I have conversations with where it's real enough that I hear the messages and understand what he's saying. It's not some made up chit-chat in my head, either. I can do that and know what I'm doing, but with him, through meditation and allowing myself to be open enough to listen to the messages, I get guidance, comfort, and reassurance about whatever it is that I'm going through at the time.

When I'm writing, I'll call upon Archangel Gabriel, the angel of communication and arts, and ask for the perfect words to share the message that I am trying to get across (like I am right now). Then I close my eyes and let the words flow. That's channeled writing, and I've been doing it my entire life except now I know what I'm doing and how to let her in. Sometimes, she'll send ideas to me when I'm stuck. I used to think I had some brilliant flash of inspiration and be all smug like it was my genius creation but now I know it's her being my muse and giving me what I need.

The other day I was lying in bed, battling a head cold and feeling like shit, thinking about this book and how to share the messages I need to share. Months had passed since that phone call where I found out about the last death which became the catalyst for me to write this book. Death lingered back of my mind as I closed my eyes for a nap; my heart rate was nice and calm, my body ready to rest and fight the germs, when out of nowhere I heard, "Conversations with...".

I sat up and looked around, my heart pounding, and I wondered if the cold meds were kicking in before realizing it was Archangel Gabriel who was talking to me.

"Conversations with WHO??!!" I yelled, sitting up and looking around the room, listening for a response. The whir of the fan beside me hummed quietly but other than that there was nothing. I laid back down, suspicious about what I had heard but knew better than to question my sanity, so I closed my eyes and thought, "OK, if you want to be a little clearer on that message, I'm listening."

Nothing came to me, so I sat with the unfinished message for a couple of days before I understood what it meant.

7 tips to get through grief

Let's just get this stuff out of the way, shall we?

1. **Boundaries**
Suffering isn't something most people like others to see them go through. Death brings out every emotion possible, sometimes to the extreme. Lean on others when you need to, check on someone who's going through it when you can, and allow boundaries to be set without taking anything personally

2. **Don't say this shit!**
"At least they went quickly. Bad for you, good for them." (Geezus balls, don't ever say this!)

"They're in a better place." (This isn't the time for your spiritual bullshit right now, Susan!)

"You'll get through it." (Sensitivity training, people!)

"You're so strong!" (Gives the impression that if they don't stay strong, they can't break when they need to)

"Are you OK?" (no, they're not OK, WTF?)

Try this instead:
Just listen. If you need to say something, offer to be there for support or respond with empathy. Having a conversation with someone who just lost a loved one can be uncomfortable but speak from the heart. You can't go wrong with that.

3. There is no linear timeline for the grieving process

Depending on which experts you talk to, there are multiple stages of grief. However, no cookie cutter process fits everyone. Steps can include (not in any definitive order):

> Denial
> Anger
> Sadness
> Acceptance
> Bargaining
> Depression
> Shock

And this: WTAF stage (what the actual fuck?)

> Why is this happening? This can't be happening? Who decided it was their time?
>
> How could God (whatever higher power you subscribe to) take this person?

You intellectually understand that the person you love is no longer with you and rationalize the event, but it's important to watch when the emotion hits you. That's when the healing begins. It doesn't matter how much you know about death or how prepared you think you are; sadness can blindside anyone at any time.

All these stages can bounce from one to the other until you finally get to the acceptance which leads to moving on with your life. Even when you think you've accepted it, you might have moments of reverting to the other stages of grief. If you find yourself unable to move past any of those points, ask for help. It's not weakness, it's the strongest thing you can do.

4. It's OK to feel a sense of relief

Don't beat yourself up for feeling relieved. When you watch someone suffer through the course of an illness, there is a sense of relief that they are no longer suffering and you are no longer wondering when the death date will be. It's not something you can plan for regardless of a timeframe a doctor might have given you. Sometimes it happens sooner than expected and you're left feeling ripped off because you were supposed to have more time. It doesn't work like that, and that's where denial sets in. Sometimes death waits and gives you more time with your loved one which can lead to false hope that everything is going to be alright or catch you off guard when it happens because they've made it weeks or months past the original death date.

There is a perception of selfishness associated with watching a loved one die slowly because you just want it to be over. Just so you know, it's not selfish, and bad karma won't attack you because you felt that way. It's not that you want them to die; it's that you want the pain of watching them die to end.

5. Give yourself permission to grieve

Strength comes from allowing yourself to take moments to process your feelings and embrace your emotions. Yes, it fucking sucks that they're gone, and no, it isn't fair that death took them from you.

Death doesn't happen to force you to move forward. You can stop and sit with your grief without doing much else. Sometimes it helps to stay busy so that you aren't consumed by the grief but that can avoidance of processing emotions. Don't bury your feelings and expect them to disappear. That's not healing, it's denial.

6. **You're not alone in your grief**

Chances are the person who died touched many lives including yours. Everyone will process death differently depending on the relationship they had with that person, and everyone is entitled to grieve the way they need to. What works for you might not work for the other person. Some people find comfort in comforting others while others need to internalize their feelings and deal with the loss without thinking of how it has impacted the people around them. Take care of your needs. That's not self-centred, it's self-care.

7. **Cry when you need to**

You don't prove how strong you are after losing someone by burying emotions because that pain you push down will manifest later on in the form of self-sabotage, rage, and pushing people away. Release the feelings you feel as you feel them.

If you're angry, vent it out or hit the gym.

If you're sad, cry and let yourself collapse into a heap until you've released that moment of grief.

If you're in shock, sit there and let yourself stay frozen for a minute.

If you have a happy memory, let it wash over you as if it's happening and feel the joy they brought to your life.

1

Not everyone survives the darkness

Dearest Tamara,

Had I known then what I know now about your journey, and the horrors you were living, I think we would have had a stronger relationship.

Looking back at our junior high days, I still remember the moment I first saw you. You had an expression of hatred towards the world, especially towards me. I can recognize now that I was not able to see the underlying hurt you were experiencing. At the time, you just came across as an angry girl with a chip on her shoulder.

I felt mostly defeated during that time, specifically with our relationship. I never understood why you hated me so much.

As time went on I remember being surprised and frustrated that our interests were so similar; we both loved 50's & 60's music, movies and even liked the same boys. Do you remember the year-

end party we had at the Waterpark, Grade 8 I think, where the slide attendant, Sandy, flirted with us? I remember looking at you in your swimsuit with your curves and much more developed body and was so envious.

Earlier that year I had travelled down east to see my ailing grandfather and brought back little souvenirs for our group of friends. I bought a small ceramic mask for you because you collected them. I remember painstakingly inspecting each one in the aisle looking for the perfect piece, hoping to please you. When I presented this token to you, I remember you accepting it with a very underwhelmed expression and a roll of your eyes. At that moment, I was once again left feeling defeated.

I suppose at the time I internalized my relationship with you, believing there were things about me that made you or others not want to be my friend. Heck, I still find myself to be a lonely, insecure, sensitive girl with few friends, now single for five years and struggling to find out who I am.

What I do know is that I have more love, admiration, and respect for you today than I ever thought possible.

I am grateful for having had these experiences with you. It's been wonderful witnessing who we've become as we grown up over the years.

I don't see you now the way I saw you back then.

Love,
Bernice

Well, fuck.

I was an asshole.

In junior high, I had a group of friends who turned out to be the only group of friends I've ever had. We did everything together: went to movies, giggled about boys, fought over who was going to marry Patrick Swayze after seeing *Dirty Dancing*, had sleepovers, and shared almost all our secrets. We were on the volleyball team, competed for the best grades, argued over whether Bon Jovi was hot or not, and rarely did anything without making sure the entire group was together.

Those girls saved my life by tolerating my extreme mood swings and putting up with my temper. If they had rejected me back then, I have no idea if I would have gotten out of the inner city. We kept each other focused on getting good grades and reminding ourselves that there was more to life than what we saw around us. They were the only people in the world I felt safe with other than my grandma. All of the girls in our circle were dealing with something at the time, but none of us ever talked about what was going on inside our homes. Bernice was in that group of friends, and the only thing I remember was that I didn't like her. I didn't have a reason for not being nice to her other than I was a stupid girl who projected her pain onto others. It's funny. I've never thought of myself as a mean person although I have a dark side that was amplified by the circumstances of my life. I can't fault my 12-year-old self for being mean but seeing those words in her letter reminded me of how my actions have impacted others.

The summer we were going into Grade 8 was when our group vowed to be pals forever. That was the summer *Stand By Me* came out, and it was like watching the boy version of my friends on screen except I saw a little of myself in each character (even Vern, although I couldn't relate to his innocence and naivety). Vern, in fact, annoyed the shit outta me. He was the friend they tolerated, kinda like the way my friends put up with me. *Stand By Me* resonated because those kids were our age, living on the wrong side of the tracks and at a crossroads in their lives. I connected with their loyalty to each other and how they paired off and had side conversations.

Stand By Me became the movie that will forever be linked with that time in my life. Like Gordie LaChance, I wanted to be a writer but felt like it was a stupid waste of time. Like Chris Chambers, I felt judged because of how poor we were and the criminal activities of those around me. And just like Teddy Duchamp, I felt this insane loyalty to a man who abused me in the worst way possible.

It was during this time that death first successfully captured my attention.

<u>Dear diary,</u>

My grandma got me this book for my 10th birthday, and I've been waiting for a reason to write in it. I'm 12 now and wish I had something better to tell you, but I don't know who else to talk to. Uncle Darrell died, so that sucks. Mom isn't taking it very well. Grandma is so sad.

Her and grampa had to come home from Kuwait (they live there because grampa works for an oil company, no idea what that means but it sounds fancy). Anyway, they came home for the funeral, but grampa doesn't seem like he wants to be here. Him and Darrell didn't get along very well. They used to fight all the time. I remember one Christmas. Uncle punched him so hard that he fell into the tree and knocked it over. When they fought like that it made me sad. Everyone was swearing and yelling, and the police came. The police always came over. I'm so sick of this.

Anyway, now that he's dead, I don't know what to do. What happens when people die? Do they go to heaven? Would he even be let in? He did a lot of bad things, but I don't think he was a bad person. Maybe it's just me, but if there is a God, he should probably look past the stuff uncle Darrell did and let him in. Gramma says he is with the angels. Not sure I believe that, either. When I would stay at her house, she had a picture of an angel looking over a little boy and girl. She said the kids in the picture were me and my brother and that we were always protected. I like that idea.

I do know that being dead means he's not coming back. Mom asked me if I wanted to go to the funeral but I do not want to remember him like that. She said he told her that if he died, he wanted to be buried face down so the world could kiss his ass goodbye (I probably shouldn't write that word but it is kind of funny. Not really.) I guess people die. (One day they're just gone.

I wish my gramma would just stay home. If she stayed here, I could go and stay with her. I don't want to stay home anymore. I need to get out of here but I have nowhere to go.

Anyway, I gotta go.

Tamara

Not every soulmate comes into your life wrapped in love and light, bearing gifts of joy and wonder or is a connection you instantly recognize. It's easy to look back after they've left your life and go, "Ah, yeah! Totally see it now!" but sometimes it takes decades before you understand why they were a part of your life and how they helped shape who you've become.

When I reached out to Bernice to write a letter for the book, I wasn't sure what to expect because even though we reconnected thanks to

Facebook, we haven't spent much time together, and I didn't realize the extent of the pain I caused her back then. We spend so much of our lives inside our bubbles, dealing with our world and never really thinking about how our words or actions can influence someone else's journey. Who I was then is obviously not who I am now, but I know that I had to be that person and experience this life to grow into the woman I am today.

It's easy to look back on your life and see the moments where things changed for you. At 12, I had no idea what death was or how pivotal that time in my life would be. After my uncle died, people in my family started dropping off like flies. It was really fucking weird. One year, six relatives died in three months, all from different causes including drug overdoses, cancer, suicide, and murder. They were violent and tragic deaths, and my grandma told me that death came in threes, so it made sense that six people died, however, I wasn't surprised when a couple more relatives passed away.

Thinking back to being 12 years old and losing my uncle, I can't say I suffered a lot of heartbreak, but I do remember thinking that he stuck around as a guardian angel, watching over me as a protector. That's the kind of guy he was in life; fiercely protective of the people he loved despite the darkness that consumed him. Sure, he was a criminal who was in and out of what my mom referred to as "Crowbar Hotel," but that didn't mean he was a bad person. He made some stupid mistakes and bad choices, but he was more than that. Even at 12 years old, I could see through the mean streak he had, straight to his soul. Maybe we were so connected because we were both Scorpios whose lives had to go through darkness and pain to see the light but he never got through it while he was here.

Not everyone survives the darkness.

I get that now.

Back then, I had no clue about death or soulmates because I was learning to survive.

I can't change the past or take back how I treated someone, however, I can continue to operate from my highest place of love and hopefully keep ascending into the best spiritual badass I can be. I never had a group of friends like the ones I had back then, and although we don't see each other in real life these days, I'll remember them forever.

Hey,

I've been thinking about you for a while, and I wanted to let you know that you're not alone.

I know you're going through some things even though you won't tell anyone. I know how much it sucks to lose Darrell, but it will teach you a few lessons you don't want to learn, and I promise, you'll be OK. I also know how much you loved your uncle and not going to the funeral was probably a good decision on your part.

Do you remember when he took you on a motorcycle ride and you thought for sure you were going to crash? Then you gave him shit for driving so dangerously, but he just laughed and winked at you, saying, "I am dangerous." And remember that time he was dropped off on the front porch at 2 a.m. after being shot in the leg, something about a drug deal gone bad? The next morning, he told you he would live forever because death couldn't touch him. Guess he was wrong.

There were so many times when he would call from jail, and he sounded so ... I don't know, alone, desperate, and completely sad. He lived a hard life, so I guess it shouldn't have been a surprise when he died from a drug overdose. He was only 27 years old. I know that sounds ancient because you're 12, but it is not. Your grandma is devastated because she lost a son, your mom is heartbroken because she couldn't save her brother and you have never lost anyone so close to you, but I'm not sure how you're coping. You saw through the tough exterior he presented and loved him even though he could be scary sometimes.

Remember that machete he called Chopper? Oh man, I almost forgot about that! If you were a brat, he'd growl,

"Where's my CHOPPER!!??" and chase you around the house lol oh man, that was funny but not really. The thing is, as mean as he could be and even though he had been in and out of jail most of his life, he never would have hurt you. He loved you more than you probably realize.

Try not to remember the sad stuff because it will make you miserable. Instead, you should think about those two scorpion tattoos that he had on his hands. Sure, they were jail tats, but he had them done for you and him because you're both Scorpios. He saw that as a special connection you between you and eventually you'll come to realize how much it meant. Those tattoos were pretty badass, just like he was.

If you think back far enough, this isn't the first time someone you know has died, but it is the first time you're aware of it, probably because your mom

41

and grandma are such a mess right now. That, and you're left to take care of things at home which sucks. You've got too much to deal with and far too many secrets for such a young girl. I need you to know that things are going to get worse for you before they get better. You've got a long road ahead, but I promise it will all be OK. Even when you think you won't get through it, you will because, just like Darrell, you're badass, too.

Death is all around you, and you don't even realize it. You think your fascination with Salem's Lot is because of the vampires, but subconsciously you are beginning your journey with understanding death. Rewatch Stand By Me. I know you love the movie because of the friendship and loyalty, but there's the underlying theme of death which ties it all together.

One day, years later, you'll see it.

And those friends you have right now, well, you'll never have another group of friends like that... It's too bad you don't realize it. You'll look back at that time as one of the most significant moments in your life, and those girls are the ones who got you through.

You should thank them. They were there for you when no one else was.

Love,

Me

The Lesson:

We don't choose our soulmates.

You might not recognize a soulmate until after they've left but when you understand why they've come into your life, you can heal wounds that you might never have realized needed attention.

When you look back on a relationship after it ends, you can recognize the moments in your life which changed the direction of the path that you were on, and the soulmates who were with you along the way. When I reflect upon my life and think about the group of friends I had in Junior High, I see them now as the soulmates they were, and know now that we were put together in that classroom for reasons we didn't understand at the time. I loved those girls. Even though I didn't show Bernice the same affection I showed the others, the love I have for her now is stronger than in junior high because I am a stronger person. I wish nothing but love for all five friends who were in my life at that time whether I see them now or not.

There's something to be said about acknowledging the past and moving forward with no remorse or regrets. Friendships are sometimes more potent than a family bond because you choose your pals. They often become better relationships than those of people you feel obligated to keep in your life. However, you don't point at someone in class or a grocery store and say, "You there! You're my soulmate, and we've crossed paths for a reason! Let's find out why!"

Let's get one thing crystal clear: you won't love every soulmate. In fact, you will despise a few of them because not all soulmates sprinkle glitter and magically make everything better. Some of your most intense soul connections are through soulmates who bring out the worst in you and cause you the most pain.

I know what you're thinking.

Why the actual shit would a soulmate be someone who hurts you?

Sorry to destroy the fairytale idea that soulmates are these mystical creatures who make your heart race and head float like a helium balloon. Some, not all, soulmates blindside you with their presence. You won't anticipate their existence, and you won't have any control over their connection in your life because they are there to teach you something. You can hate them, be angry with them, feel the pain inflicted by them and do everything you can to cut them out of your life but there's a reason they have come to you at this point. **Who you were before a soulmate comes into your life and who you become after they leave will be two very different versions of yourself.** Death isn't the way these soulmate connections end, either. There is an ending to the relationship however that leaves the opportunity for them to come back into your life unless you energetically sever the cords. If you are emotionally attached to someone, you are connected to them through energy because you're feeding them through emotion. Love, anger, resentment, joy, sadness. If you are attaching any of these to how you feel about someone, you are connected and haven't learned what they came to teach you.

7 types of soulmates

Rose and Jack's love story on *Titanic* was the kind of romantic soulmate connection that we look for in a relationship. He unexpectedly came into her life, and they saw a future together despite the odds stacked against them. Just when she takes a leap of faith to be with him, the damn ship hits an iceberg, and that's the end of that. However, it's the beginning of her new life. Hollywood has created some beautifully tragic love stories that have shaped our idea of what a soulmate is, and although it's true that a soulmate can be romantic, not all connections are lifelong nor are they the fairytale we had always imagined.

Not every soulmate fits into a box. You'll find some of your soulmates blend in some of these categories. This section isn't meant to place your relationships in a tidy little package; it's to show how soulmates can enter into your life through these types of connections.

Friend:
- ➤ They listen
- ➤ Don't judge your bad decisions
- ➤ Tell you the ugly truth especially when you don't want to hear it
- ➤ Love you even when they hate what you say or do

> You can pick up where you left off whether it's weeks, months or years
> Don't always stay in your life but when they are there, the moments cause a shift in the path that you're on or change you in some way
> See something in you that no one else looks for

Antagonist:

> Cause pain that ends up being a lesson you needed to ascend to another level
> Bring out the worst in you
> Force you to confront your shadow side, the darkest fears and gloomy parts of your soul
> Bring about considerable change to your life through showing your strength to overcome adversity and become resilient
> Stay in your life until you learn the lessons you need to learn. It is possible to severe your energetic attachment to completely remove them from this lifetime
> They shake up your world through chaotic encounters
> Who you were before they came into your life is not who you will be once they're gone

Blood:

> Family members (mom, dad, siblings, grandparents) who have a role in your life are soulmates

> Your soul decides what journey it will take before it enters into this lifetime and that includes who your parents will be. This applies to your children whether you birth them or not

> Just like other soulmate relationships, you are not obligated to keep these people in your life if they bring negativity or pain. Learn what you can and try to do what's best for your life. It's not selfish to end relationships if it causes you more pain to be connected than it does to let go even when the person is related to you.

> If you can remember that you chose this lifetime and this family, it helps you understand why these people are in your life.

> They give you a greater understanding of the soul lessons you need to learn and why they are immediately in your life instead of randomly showing up throughout your journey

Transient:

> ➤ These connections are brief yet memorable

> ➤ Interactions with a Transient Soulmate happen by chance and are gone just as quickly as they appear

> ➤ Messages from these soulmates are often profound and what you need to hear at that moment, affirm what you already know or make you think twice about a decision you were about to make

> ➤ You feel instantly connected to the person like you've known them before

> ➤ Paths cross momentarily, but the conversation sticks with you or pops up as a flashback when something happens to remind you of them

> ➤ You meet as strangers and leave as strangers, rarely do you encounter these soulmates more than once in a lifetime

Course-correction:

> Teachers, coaches, mentors or anyone whose guidance helps direct you on your path
> This isn't about career or education; these people are soul teachers who help you understand the bigger picture
> They help you along your healing journey and share wisdom they've learned along the way

Sexual:

> These are first loves, affairs, marriages and other intimate relationships that open your eyes to understanding what you need from a partner
> These soulmates often bring you to a greater awareness of who you are looking for in a love connection
> They help you discover who you want to connect with through your relationship with them
> Not all intimate connections are soulmates. Don't mistake a soulmate for a sex partner

Love:

- ➢ You can have more than one in your lifetime
- ➢ Initially, you can't stand the thought of physically being apart from them (as relationships bloom, day-to-day shit builds and you can forget how this feels)
- ➢ Your soul recognizes their soul even if you can't explain why you feel so connected to them
- ➢ You've been together in other lifetimes
- ➢ Even if you don't stay together for the rest of this lifetime, your souls will find each other in the next one
- ➢ They help you heal, grow and ascend into higher vibrations of yourself
- ➢ They can leave and come back throughout your lifetime if there is unfinished business

2

"I don't love you
and I'm not sure I ever did."

Soundtrack

Yes, there is an official playlist for *Love*. These songs are tied to memories and you can follow on my Spotify account: YouAreFIERCE.

Here's a peek:

Pain Three Days Grace
Don't Turn Around Ace of Base
Never Ever All Saints
New Orleans is Sinking Tragically Hip
Back 2 Life Soul II Soul
November Rain Guns 'n' Roses
I Remember You Skid Row
Creep TLC
Shy Guy Diana King
Twisted Keith Sweat
Unbreak My Heart Toni Braxton
When Doves Cry Ginuine
Do What You Have to Do Sarah McLachlan
Here Without You 3 Doors Down
Scars Papa Roach
Walk Away Christina Aguilera
Paradise By the Dashboard Light Meatloaf
Fastlove George Michael
I Hate Everything About You Three Days Grace
In the End Linkin Park
I Get Off Halestorm
There You Go Pink

Almost every Eminem song

Dear diary,

I get it now. <u>People leave whether they want to or not!!</u>

They die. Relationships end. No one stays in your life

long enough for you to be happy and if you ever get to the

point where you are happy, the universe will take it away

because you don't fucking deserve it!!!

You know what I was doing the day I found out my

grandma had cancer? Having sex for the first time

because I'm selfish. Instead of going to see her or my

mom, I lost my virginity. I knew she was going to die, but

I decided to not care about her needs and satisfied my

own instead.

I feel alone. I can't turn to my family for anything

because it's not like my mom ever had her shit together in

the first place. My grandma died in my grandpa's

arms, did you know that? My uncle called to tell me

and my mom picked me up to see my grandpa, but he didn't want to talk to anyone. I didn't expect her to die. I didn't expect that call. I don't know what I expected but she wasn't supposed to die so soon. She died almost exactly a year to the day she found out she had cancer.

Of everything I've been through this year, the toughest thing I've had to deal with was losing my grandma. I keep thinking she's just a phone call away but that's not true. She was the only one who was always there for me no matter what and now she's gone.

I'm pretty sure I'll be alone forever. I don't have anyone left I can't count, not even my mom because let's face it: I haven't been able to rely on her since she gave birth to me. I can't lean on my grandpa because he's a million miles away and has to deal with his grief.

And this whole breaking up/getting back together

with my boyfriend sucks. I wonder if I'll ever find true love or someone who will love me unconditionally or be loved by anyone for any reason.

I'll never forget the first time he told me he loved me. That was the happiest day of my life. And then there was the day that he told me he didn't love me anymore and wasn't sure if he ever did. And now that we're together again, I feel as though I'm losing him. Each day, I find myself falling for him all over again, but it scares me. I don't want to be in love if I'm going to get hurt and I'm afraid that if I let myself get too close, nothing will work out. I can't lose him again so soon after my grandma died. I can't take that kind of heartbreak!!.

Who the fuck have I become?? This isn't me. I'm not weak. I'm tough. I survived all those years at home, and I'm going to do something with my life. So why am I so unhappy?? Why can't I be happy?? Oh wait I know. Because every time I AM HAPPY, someone dies or leaves.

Does everyone go through this much shit by the time they're 19?? I'm only 19. Why does life have to be so fucking mean??

I've got to toughen up again. Be like Dally Winston from The Outsiders. "When you're tough, nothing can touch you!" Yeah, that's my new motto. Words to live by. I should get that saying tattooed on my ass.

I gotta go. I have to figure out what to do with my life.

T.

I can't remember the first time I saw him, but I'll never forget the last time we spoke. It was years after we broke up and he had become a faded memory, a chapter in my story, and nothing more. He hadn't even crossed my mind in recent years, but for some reason, without a memory trigger, he consumed my thoughts.

I blame Mercury Retrograde for reconnecting us. That's what happens during Mercury Retrograde: people from your past pop into your present to remind you of something you needed to learn but didn't. Facebook is great for finding people from your past, and that's precisely how we reconnected. One stupid message after the other, reaching out to see how the other person was doing and suddenly the vortex of my past sucked me into its chaos. Memories swirled around me like I was reliving 1990 something only this time, I was the observer searching for the lesson instead of desperately trying to cling to someone who didn't love me anymore.

When I was a teenager it seemed like every couple of months someone I knew, died. A high school friend of mine committed suicide, my mom's cousin died of an overdose, my grandma's older sister died from cancer, a handful of cousins passed away, and my great grandma died at the ripe old age of 82.

It never seemed to end.

Their deaths didn't change me in any grand way. I became consumed with holding onto a relationship that I thought would never end and too wrapped up in my emotional turmoil to realize my grandma's death was right in front of me.

A couple of months before she passed away, right after her sister died, I had a dream that shook me to my core. I was sharing a studio apartment with my grandma at the time and had decided to take a nap while she had coffee with my mom. As I slept, I heard knocking at the door and woke up to answer it. My aunt was standing there, looking like she did when she was in her 20s with a bouffant hairstyle and blue eyeshadow.

"Uhm. What are you doing here?" I asked, not sure if I was awake or asleep.

"Tell your grandma that it's OK," she said.

"What? What the hell does that mean?!"

"Tell her everything will be OK. It's beautiful here."

I started to panic, my heart heavy with grief and wondered what the hell a dead relative was doing at my door. I was confused and weirded out and sat up in bed, drenched in sweat. I could hear my mom and grandma chatting away on the other side of the divider. Shaking my head and wiping my eyes, I got up and pulled the divider open. They both looked up at me and stopped their conversation.

"What's wrong, my girl?" my mom asked.

"You look whiter than usual," my grandma said, chuckling. "Bad dream?"

I looked at them both and said, "I had a dream about Aunty Carol. She had this beehive hairdo and bad makeup, and she said to tell you it was OK."

My grandma went still and held her breath. The colour drained from her face, and she asked, "What did you say?"

"She told me to tell you that it's OK," I replied. "Whatever the hell that means. She said it's beautiful and that it's OK."

I was still trying to rationalize how a dream could feel so real and wanted to dismiss it.

"That wasn't a dream, Tamara," she said. The look of concern on my grandma's face was enough to tell me there was something more prominent than I understood had happened.

"A few years ago, we were having coffee late one night, and we made a deal that whoever died first had to come back and tell the other one what it was like."

I felt like someone punched me in the stomach. "What?"

"She came to you. That wasn't a dream," my grandma replied. "She came to you to give me a message. You have a gift."

"You're crazy. That isn't a thing. Dead people don't come back and talk to you!"

"It runs in the family, Tamara. You're not the only one who is in touch with the other side."

No way, I thought. That was a dream. No fucking way were dead relatives coming to visit me. I wouldn't have it. My grandma was clearly suffering from some radiation-induced insanity.

"Sure, whatever," I replied, unable to shake the feeling of how real that dream was.

Not long after that dream, my grandma died in my grandpa's arms. Regret settled over me like a warm blanket and I hated myself for not being there for her.

Why didn't I spend more time with her?

Why didn't I ask her questions about my mom?

Why didn't I write everything down that she ever told me?

Why didn't I appreciate her while she was here??

That was the first time death made me feel anything, and I didn't know what to do. With her passing, I had no one left in my life who could guide me. No one. Not only did I lose my grandma but my heart was broken once again when my boyfriend broke up with me shortly after she passed away. It was then that I decided you can't have love without pain.

About a year after she died, I dreamt that I was at her funeral and there was a viewing of the body. I was saying goodbye without looking at her, but people kept telling me to kiss her before she left. I refused, but then she was beside me and said, "I'll always be with you, Tamara."

I hugged her and begged her not to go. "I still need you in my life," I said, tears streaming down my face. Sobs racked my body, and I woke up in tears, clutching my pillow and wishing she was still there. She was there, I felt it. I knew her spirit was with me, but she wasn't physically there for me to hug and tell her how much I loved her. The pain felt as fresh as the night she died, and I didn't know how to stop it.

"I'm here for you if you need me."

"Thanks, but I'm good. You're the one who needs me," I replied. "I love you. I don't care if those are the last words I ever say to you just as long as you hear me."

"I hear them, and I love you, too."

The Lessons:

The love you have for someone never really disappears; it's merely forgotten and evaporates into nothingness becoming invisible to the mind's eye but never to the soul's energy.

This philosophy applies to death and broken relationships.

I found a couple of journals I had kept from that time in my life. Flipping through the pages, I didn't recognize myself in the somber prose of a broken young girl, but flashes of those memories came back. I read through the books, word for word, feeling my head spin with memories long buried; fragmented moments in time clumsily finding their way together like a weak magnetic puzzle that made no sense. I read both diaries three times over before I could put the pieces together. Random names of friends whose faces I couldn't visualize became characters in a story I barely remember the details of, but this journal captured what seemed to be one of the most monumental moments in my life. The relationships I had then will forever be tied to the memory of my grandma's death.

As a kid, you never really knew heartbreak until your heart breaks from the death of a first love's commitment.

Pages of regret over failed relationships and wishes for finding true love, all very pathetic musings of someone who had no idea how to focus on what mattered, filled the ragged books. Everything I was going through at that time, the heartache, the grief and the lack of direction for my future was a blessing in disguise even though I didn't see it that way.

That's what happens with grief; you never see it as a new beginning because the ending consumes you. When darkness envelopes and squeezes the faith right out of you, a glimmer of hope will suddenly flicker in the distance and bring you to your knees in gratitude. You finally feel like there's a way out. Rarely do we ever take the time while immersed in despair to search for the lessons; instead, we freeze out of fear or flail out of necessity, trying to grasp at anything or for anyone who can save us. The reality is, the only person who can save you is you.

A thousand hands can reach out to you, and a thousand voices can tell you the messages you need to hear, but until you're ready to accept that help and listen to the messages, no one can carry you through a healing journey. Those are steps you need to take with your own two feet.

Soulmates don't have to die for the relationship to end. Most times, it's because what they've come to teach and learn has finished, they can no longer help you ascend and have gotten you as far in your journey as possible.

Whether it's death or heartbreak that separates you, the lessons you carry with you are what shape who you become and what you do with your life.

There's something special about your first love, something magical that makes you romanticize it years later even when you've moved on. That's when you start reflecting on the 'what ifs' and ponder what might have been but let me tell you the fantasy is always better than the reality.

When I reconnected with my ex-boyfriend, I had to wonder why he had come back into my life? Did I still love him? I had loved him then and realized I always would, but I was not *in love* with him now. The love I felt was one that bound us energetically and I know that he popped back into my life because he needed me and I needed to learn something from him.

It took a whole lot of searching for the answers, but I finally understood that soulmates come in and out of your life throughout this journey. Some stay forever, but most leave when their soul reconnects with another soulmate, and the energy of your connection can temporarily flip the off switch. Sometimes they come back, and when they do, there is a valuable lesson to be learned. It doesn't mean that the love reignites, but it provides the opportunity for additional healing. Try to figure out what you need to learn or what you haven't released then grow from it. It's OK to be sad when the universe hits the off switch once again, but it's easier to let go when you know it's not forever, just part of the journey.

You have multiple soulmates who will come into your life when you need them and leave when they've taken you as far as they can in the time that they have with you. You can't blame them. They have a journey, too, and most times it has nothing to do with you because where they end up is where they need to be.

Mitchell's story

I started taking Uber recently but don't usually chat with the driver because I'm buried in work or have been working on this book. One trip was with Mitchell who, within a five-minute drive from point A to point B, told me he had recently lost his mom. She was 99 years old. I told him I was sorry to hear of his loss, but he smiled and said he was OK.

About a month later, I was waiting for my Uber and Mitchell appeared. I asked how he was doing since our last conversation and he said, "Didn't I tell you? I had the most amazing experience right after she passed." Being in the final stages of writing this book, I was curious as to what he had to say since death seemed to be lurking in the shadows once again.

"The hospital called me at 3:15 in the afternoon to tell me my mom had just passed away. I said, 'OK,' and I cried. I just fell over onto the couch and fell asleep, which I don't usually do.

"All of a sudden, I was walking down this beautiful road, it looked like I was in the country but I'd never seen such a beautiful place. Out of nowhere, my mom and dad came walking out of this path and both my parents looked like they were in their 30s. My mom had her brown hair and my dad, who had already passed away, looked like he did when he was younger. My mom said, 'Mitchell, look at how nice it is here! And we're not old!'

"Oh, the feeling I had when I was there with them!" he

continued. "I said, 'Mom this place is so beautiful!' She said, 'Yes!' and she held my dad's hand. He never spoke, only my mom did. She said, 'We're not old anymore!'

"That always bothered my mom, that she was old," he clarified.

I asked Mitchell what it felt like to be there and he replied, "It was like I was injected with peace. It was so superb that I didn't want it to stop. She said, 'Your little girl is here' that we lost. And she said, 'Everybody is here that passed on!' And I said, 'Really?!'

"And then I woke up and I've never grieved since that day. My mom lived with us for many years. I thought I'd be a mess (when she died). But I've never grieved since. And I've never been scared to die since then, either."

It wasn't always that way for Mitchell. Before her death, he said he would get his mind to a place of mourning, hoping the exercise would help him get through the inevitable end.

"I'd go through nights trying to pretend she died so I could grieve," he said. "She came to let me know (it would be OK)."

You can listen to the full audio clip at YouAreFIERCE.com/LoveMitchell

3

You died
and I still didn't understand
what it meant to live.

I only knew that when you left,
you had no choice.

Hey,

Fuck, I wish I could tell you it's going to get easier, but the truth is, you're going to live with this for the rest of your life. You will have sparks of joy that will come to you in various forms but never enough to ignite a change within you until you're ready to see everything you've gone through as a gift. Only then will you learn what this all means.

Remember the day before you found out he died? You were driving and saw the most magnificent ring of lights around the sun, and you found yourself thinking about him? And remember how, at that moment, you heard Toni Braxton's haunting voice on the radio singing, Unbreak My Heart? And how you smiled because you couldn't stop thinking of him until you realized the video for the song was about her boyfriend's death and that the lyrics were all about wanting to hear his voice just one more time? And suddenly your heart broke even though you didn't understand why? Do you remember how you started to shake and your heart pounded and all you wanted to do was get home so you could call him just to make sure he was OK but when you did, he didn't answer?

Don't leave me in all this pain, you thought, hearing the song play over and over in your head, wondering why the fuck he didn't answer and why you couldn't shake the feeling that it all meant something? He was with you then, but you just didn't know it. He was there with you, comforting you even though you didn't realize you needed comforting. He's still with you and will be with you, forever. He'll make an appearance later in your life in ways that will shake you but be open to the message because it's his way of telling you that he'll never leave your side.

All of this will eventually make sense but

right now, in this moment, all I can do is love you and watch you go through it because you're not ready to understand why it's happening. You'll get there, I promise. I know the pain you feel because I've lived it. All I can do is hold you in my heart and promise you that after all of it, all the pain and heartache, you'll look up to the stars and see the magic in your journey. <u>You're going to make it.</u>

Love,

Me

I couldn't tell you his birthday, favourite kind of cookie or even much about what he looked like; all I know is his name was Keon, and I loved him.

Love, I discovered, found you when you weren't looking for it. Before online dating was a thing, before I knew what a soulmate was and before I understood the power of the universe, he came into my life in the most unexpected and strangest way. I can't believe I'm going to confess this because looking back, I was such a dumbass but right after my grandma died, I felt so lost and searched for answers as to why people kept leaving my life. It was bad enough to have my heart broken from my first love but losing her reaffirmed that people left whether they chose to or death took them away. Anyway, ugh I still can't believe I'm fessing up to this, I became addicted to calling psychic hotlines. I would call those damn things repeatedly and ask if I would ever find true love, if my life would always be difficult, and if I would ever be happy.

I know. I KNOW!! I realize now how stupid that was but wait! It gets better.

Because I was calling these hotlines, my phone bill was higher than I could afford to pay. I was making $5.25/hour working part-time at a grocery store as a cashier and barely able to make rent and buy groceries. My phone bill ended up at a collections agency, and that's when he called me.

I was so embarrassed. The bill was for $225, and I

had to make arrangements to pay it off, but before we hung up the phone, I made some comment about how smooth his voice was. He laughed, and we ended up chatting. I didn't think much of it until we started talking every day, the conversations had nothing to do with my delinquent phone bill, and I couldn't wait to hear from him.

We shared moments of our day, talked about things we had been through, discussed the dreams we had for our future and what it would be like to eventually meet in person. I sent him a picture of a Sunshine Girl shoot I had done as a joke (my friend was a photographer for the local newspaper that printed daily photos of women, usually in bikinis. I was not in a bikini for the shot, more from my lack of self-confidence than anything else but I thought I looked good, and I wanted him to see me.) One night, about a month into our... whatever it is you want to classify it as... the conversation took a romantic turn, and we started sharing songs that expressed how we were feeling about each other.

"Girl, you got me twisted and turning," he said.

I smiled, confused and asked him what he meant by that.

"Because your heart is where my love is at," he said, quoting the song lyrics to Keith Sweat's *Twisted*.

I wasn't ready for the word "love" to come into play, but my heart melted, and I envisioned him on the other end of the phone, lying in bed and looking up at the ceiling as we spoke. We talked about the possibility of going to visit him in Toronto, meeting his family and even moving there to be with him. As much as I loved the idea, there was a part of me that wouldn't let myself get caught up in the romance. I had a vision of how my life was going to turn out and moving to Toronto wasn't a part of that plan. I didn't know what he looked like, we had never met in real life, and it didn't seem real. There was no way relationships started out like this, I thought. How could I feel so connected to someone I had never met?

"Don't think about it too much," he said. "Don't think about why it wouldn't work. Picture it, us together, and see it is real. I see it every day when I look around me. I see you here with me holding my hand, and we're together. I see it wherever I look. You have to see it, too."

After every conversation, I cautiously let myself get lost a little more in the fantasy. Maybe it could happen, I thought. It was the first time since my grandma died that I felt the slightest ray of happiness and I wanted to hold onto it.

Right before my 21st birthday, the UPS driver showed up at my door.

"What's this?!" I asked as if he would know.

He looked at the return address and said, "Someone from Toronto sent you this."

I gasped in surprise and grabbed the package. "Thank you!" I yelled before closing the door and running to the kitchen to grab a knife. As I slid the sharp end into the tape to open the box, I felt this swell of love rush over me. I ripped open the envelope and looked at the card.

"Happy birthday Tamara. Love, Keon."

I couldn't remember the last time anyone had given me a birthday present. Inside the package was a black and white striped tiger that I held close and snuggled. That night, Keon and I talked about making plans to meet, and I shyly asked him why he signed the card, 'Love, Keon.'

He took a moment before responding. "Because I think I'm falling in love with you."

I didn't know what to say. My heart felt the same, but my head kept telling me it couldn't be real. Nothing about this was normal. Normal for me was meeting some guy in a bar and deciding whether or not to give him my number. Normal wasn't some random phone call from a collections agency turning into thoughts of a different future and love for someone I'd never even seen in a photo. For a brief moment, I stopped myself from being afraid and decided to go with it.

"Oh," I replied, hoping that would be his response but it still left me breathless. The silence between us wasn't awkward or uncomfortable, but I knew I had to say something else, so I said, "I feel the same way."

"So you say you want me oooh make up your mind 'cause I'm not gonna be here for long," he once again serenaded me with *Twisted*. I smiled, burning the song into my memory, knowing that every time I heard it, I'd think of him. Before we said goodnight, I told him I had plans to go out for my birthday weekend but that I would call him on Sunday. After a weekend of overindulging with my girlfriend, I phoned, the concern weighing heavily on me from the feeling I got when I heard *Unbreak My Heart* on the radio, but there was no answer. I tried a few more times that night and even called his work the next day, but he wasn't in. Even though I tried to dismiss the feeling I had as nothing, I called his house again, but it wasn't his smooth voice who answered. It was his mom.

"Are you the girl in the picture?" she asked.

Suddenly, this feeling of complete dread washed over me. "Yes," I replied. Why is she answering his phone? Why isn't he there? Why haven't I heard from him??

"Keon died. Please, I can't talk right now," she said, handing the phone to his sister.

"Wait, why are you telling me this?" I pleaded.

His sister told me he had an epileptic reaction and choked to death on Saturday. That was two days ago, I thought. Two days ago, I was partying at a nightclub, celebrating my 21st birthday and wondering if I should give up my life here to move there to be with him or stay where I was comfortable and not take a chance at all. Just like that, the universe decided for me. I wouldn't be going anywhere because there was no longer anyone at the end of that journey.

I should have known, I thought.

I should have known better than to think something

good would come into my life, especially around my birthday. People left, they always did, whether they wanted to or had no choice. Like all the deaths before his, I had no one to talk to about what I was experiencing. The only friend I had told about him looked suspiciously at me like I was losing my mind to fall for someone I had never met. We met guys at the bar not from across the country through a stupid phone call, she said. I knew that didn't make sense and how ridiculous the whole thing was, but it felt right to me, and I couldn't make anyone else understand so I didn't bother.

I had to mourn his death alone, crying and breaking down by myself in my basement suite, sobbing and asking out loud:

Why was this happening?

Why did I have to lose someone I had never met but felt a love I couldn't explain?

Why did everyone who came into my life, leave?

What had I done to deserve this pain?

When was I ever going to be happy without expecting something bad to come along and ruin it?

Why did I keep pushing people away?

When would this pain go away?

Why did he have to die before we ever got the chance to look into each other's eyes to see if this was real?

The emotional weight I carried after his death crushed me, but I refused to let him go. I didn't understand that he was with me more now than he had ever been.

There is nothing you can say to someone in the midst of a tragedy that will bring any comfort. No one wants to hear, **"It was their time," "It all happens for a reason,"** or **"The pain won't last forever."**

Death doesn't discriminate against age, gender, religion or race and it sure as fuck doesn't care if you've accomplished what you set out to do or have unfinished business.

Death happens whether you like it or not.

I feel your love
without ever seeing you.

It's not in my head;
it's in my heart
and in my soul
which is,
and always will be,
connected to yours.

Lifetime after lifetime;

You are why
I take leaps of faith
without fearing
where I fall

The Lessons:

What's the label on a relationship like this one? Boyfriend? Friend? Let's go with soulmate because Keon was the first experience I had with a soul connection that opened my heart to trusting the sensation of love you feel for someone even though it shouldn't make sense.

This is what I knew:

I couldn't deal with his death because I didn't know how to deal with it

I was tired of being strong

I wanted to run away

I didn't know who to talk to, and I didn't want to talk about it even if I had someone to talk to

I had no idea what to do

When you lose someone you're in love with, the idea of ever loving someone again seems selfish and disrespectful to the love that you had. The truth is, if you fall in love again, the guilt you feel goes away with an understanding that he or she wouldn't hold you to a vow or commitment made on earth.

Although they will stay with you in your heart and memories, they will not physically be with you for the rest of your lifetime, and you have to continue living life while you're here.

You can't protect yourself from love forever.

Even if you vow never to love again the way you loved the person who died, love finds you through the relationships you have with your friends, children, siblings, parents or other people who are in your life that you have a heart-centric connection.

"I don't want to love anyone the way I loved him because I can't stand to feel that kind of pain again."

"People you know will die, regardless of the relationship. Does that mean it won't hurt?"

Absolutely it will hurt like fuck but holding yourself back from loving another person is giving up on life. Isolating yourself from love is the loneliest way to live, and it will be more painful than opening up your heart again.

At the time, I believed in this twisted universal law that for every good thing that happened in my life, ten bad things would happen to balance it out and because I believed it to be true, it was. Every year around my birthday from the time I was 18 to my late 30s, some challenge would present itself, I believed, as a direct result of choices I made in my life. It's like the universe decided to remind me every year that I was a bad person who needed to pay for my sins. I deserved to suffer, that much I knew, and so each year in November I came to expect the worst.

This heartache was different. Everything about Keon and me was different, and I felt the cruel hand of fate twist my heart until I couldn't even breathe. His death was another layer of pain that fed the demons I was desperately trying to starve to death through burying the pain but losing him exposed every raw emotion I had skillfully masked with indifference and rage.

Losing my grandma and my uncle did not prepare me for losing love in this form. It's one thing to lose a relative, but it's something else to lose a romantic soulmate. Not even the breakups I'd experienced could have given me a taste of what losing Keon felt like. I had no idea what a soulmate was at that point, however, I knew we had a connection. I just I couldn't explain it to anyone. The abrupt ending of it all left me confused and disoriented like I was intoxicated in a black fog and couldn't find my way out.

After all the death I'd known up to that point, you'd think I would have been able to understand loss better, but I wasn't able to cope because I was already dealing with so much trauma in my life. For me, another death only validated what I already knew to be true: people left whether they wanted to or not, I didn't deserve to be happy, and for every good thing that happened, ten bad things would balance it out.

Most adults don't know how to look at themselves and see the darkness within so how could I expect myself, at 21, to understand the pain I was projecting onto the people around me? I was blind to it because anger and sadness consumed me, and I wore it as a badge of honour.

How do you move on from that?

How do you envision a future where you're happy when all you've experienced is pain, death, and heartbreak?

What steps do you need to take to feel like you can live again without the guilt of moving on?

I didn't know how to cope, and no one around me had answers, so I had to figure it out on my own.

Here is what I learned: the boyfriends I had moved on with their lives by choice, but Keon died, and I was left to live. Even if I didn't know how I had to keep going.

Before he came into my life, I had known what my future looked like and then suddenly passed away, and everything I thought I had control over exploded in my face. It took months before I realized that opening myself up to taking a leap of faith was the only way to live my life and honour what we had.

It wasn't like flicking a light switch, and suddenly everything made sense. I felt guilty the first time I had sex after Keon died because all I could think about was how I was betraying the love I had for him. He wasn't physically there, but my heart was still connected to his, and it hurt so fucking bad that we couldn't be together. Nothing would ever be the same, I told myself. I forced myself to keep living even though I didn't want to, and it wasn't because he died. All of the whispering demons I had tried so hard to bury were getting louder and louder as the weeks rolled by after his death.

Emotions are not something you can control when someone dies no matter how hard you want to or even try. There will be times when a song plays that jolts you back to a moment you have re-lived a million times in your head, but suddenly the lyrics bring you face to face with the person you've lost. Your senses are on fire, and everything around you is real again. And just as fast, it's gone.

I began to realize that music was his way of communicating with me, letting me know he was there in my saddest moments even though I couldn't see, hear, or touch him. Keith Sweat's *Twisted* would play at the clubs as one of the night's closing songs when I felt most alone, and I'd have to leave because the tears wouldn't stop flowing. Keon died days after my 21st birthday and weeks after Toni Braxton released *UnBreak My Heart* as a single. I began searching for messages in those songs where I never noticed them before and realized that with *Twisted*, he didn't know it but he was saying he wasn't going to be in my life very long. I listened over and over, hearing key phrases like "be strong," "I'm not gonna be here for long," "reason for the pain," and "you left me all alone." They looped on repeat, and I knew he was trying to get through to me, but I wasn't ready to listen.

That's what happens when someone dies: you start grasping at conversations you had with them or replaying phrases and moments in your head hoping to cling to some message that will get you through until you see them again. Sometimes it works, and other times it's too faded for you to hear what they have to say, so you search for something to keep their spirit alive. I didn't even know I was doing it; I only knew that if I pretended like he never existed, I would suffer more than if I relived the moments we had together.

God, I loved him.

With everything I was at that time, I loved him and even now, death doesn't change anything for me. There was a purity to our connection that wasn't tainted by a day-to-day relationship which brings about petty annoyances and arguments over who should change the toilet paper roll. It doesn't make the loss more or less than someone else's pain because it's mine and I had to go through it to get through other losses and pain in my life. The whole time, he stayed with me in spirit, and I know now that his death redirected me onto this path for a reason. I am grateful for the moment we were connected but understand why it needed to end.

It's easy to see it now, but if he hadn't come into my life, I don't know that I would have learned to trust my heart and take the leaps of faith I did throughout the rest of my journey. Up to that point, and even now, I wouldn't consider myself a free spirit, someone who goes wherever the mood takes them without plotting out a course of action, however, I did learn that the steps I took to get to the result I was looking for, didn't matter. What mattered was knowing what I wanted the outcome to be and taking a step in the direction I wanted to go. That, my friends, is called trusting the universe, and even though I had no clue at the time that I was doing exactly that, I started doing just that.

People will come into your life and try to talk you out of what you know in your heart to be true whether it's when you're ready to move on from grief or when you want to go right when they think you "should" go left. They'll tell you all the reasons you'll fail. You know you should try.

I didn't know how to move on after Keon died. When the grief became something I could no longer hide, people would question why I was so sad, and when I told them, the blank looks would remind me why I didn't want to tell people in the first place. None of my friends could relate because no one I knew had lost someone they loved.

Love is love and when you lose it whether it's through death or a breakup, the part of you that dies with it never really ends; it merely fragments into a piece of the mosaic which becomes the beautiful masterpiece of your life. Your memories, tragedies, triumphs, tears, and turmoil recreate this version of you. It's not fragile or flawed, and it doesn't have to be reminders of the worst moments you've endured.

I see this ascension as a resurrection that rises wrapped in the ashes of what you've lost. That delicate residue becomes the glue that binds those moments together like a glorious kintsugi monument to your life. You are everything that has happened to you, good and bad, but that's not where your story ends. You can't pretend you didn't lose someone you loved or that their life didn't impact your journey, but you can move forward without them. Staying stuck in time is a choice, but life will go on with or without you participating.

I started living again by simply going through the motions because I had no choice. I couldn't give up or stay in bed because I had bills to pay and obligations to show up to jobs I hated. Maybe that mundane routine saved me but I was alone in my recovery, and I had no choice but to keep moving forward.

Love doesn't mean suffering when you're mourning the death of someone you loved but the shock, pain, numbness, and refusal to believe they're gone, is your reality. There's no right way or easy way to recover but **when you learn to live, you create moments that become the building blocks for your future based on the experiences of your past.**

How do you feel when someone close to you dies suddenly?
Well, everyone reacts differently and the reaction depends on a couple of things:

How close were you?

What kind of soulmate were they?

What do you believe about death?

Have you ever lost someone close to you before this?

When death knocks you on your ass and takes away someone you love without the courtesy of letting you say goodbye, it's a big fucking deal. Not only did you not get to say a final "I love you" or end the relationship on your terms, but you're left dissecting everything you've said to that person while they were here. Regrets begin to surface, guilt unintentionally and wickedly manifests, desperation rises to the surface, and all you want to know is WHY the fuck they died so suddenly?

The spiritual response is that their time on earth ended. Comforting as a cactus up the ass, right? It doesn't matter if their time was up, their journey was over, and they completed everything they had set out to do because when death interferes with our lives because that is not the message you want to hear. You want more time with them and the chance to say goodbye and to let them know how much you love them.

Not physically having someone in your life doesn't mean that you can't have conversations with them.

Death is a temporary separation

The spirit hangs around for a while after death. If you're open enough, you can feel their presence. Sometimes they give you a sign that they're near with a song that pops into your head or on the radio, or a scent that appears out of nowhere, or just that feeling you get when someone enters a room (that's energy, baby!). So when you're in desperate need of conversation with them, start talking. Yell, cry, swear, breakdown, get everything off your chest and know that they can hear you whether you see them or not. Having a conversation with someone who isn't there doesn't make you insane, by the way; it's a way to work through your grief and release some of the remorse you feel over words left unspoken or broken pieces you can't put back together. For the record, it's probably best that you do this in private, not in your local Starbucks with everyone looking at you like you ARE crazy.

Regardless of what you believe, what faith you follow or what your views are on life and death, when someone dies, it feels like the universe is saying, "Fuck you and your desire to be happy!" The universe doesn't talk that way, but it feels like it.

You will be OK eventually, but you must allow every

single awful feeling to rise to the surface, feel it as painfully as it is going to feel, and start releasing it. This isn't easy, either. There is an ebb and flow of feelings, like the tide in a storm, coming to shore in powerful waves then reluctantly retreating to the ocean, easing up on the pressure. Eventually, as you allow yourself to feel and deal with what you can handle, the intensity is eroded, and the layers of pain begin to wear thin as you heal and time passes. This delicate scar tissue builds up, binding you together and reminding you of the life that was lost and the strength you had to endure it.

There is no linear grief process.

Emotions can go from shock to anger to denial back to anger to sadness to numbness to acceptance back to rage. Whatever you feel is yours to experience, and no one can tell you what to expect.

Death comes for all of us; the people we love and the people you'll never meet. Don't expect grief to be easy because it never is regardless of what you believe or who you've lost before. **Death fucking sucks.** You always want more time or one last conversation, but it doesn't work that way.

The thing about death is that once you've experienced it, you never want to go through it again. You can start to look at your relationships with fear and anxiety, thinking about losing them and become paralyzed by fear of letting yourself love someone.

Sometimes the pain we feel after losing someone is

projected onto others in the form of hate not because we genuinely despise people but because of the brokenness we feel inside.

"I'm never going to find love because no one will ever love me for who I am."

"That's only true because you believe it's true."

"I am a realist. That's my reality."

"You create your reality."

4

From the ashes
of your disaster
rises the most
resilient
and beautiful of souls

You are love

You got this

Dear Tamara,

If memory serves, the first day we met was when you bounced into my store all smiles and friendly as fuck. I'm not sure entirely how our relationship evolved, but it started as a business venture. My retail partner and I bought ads from your magazine. We became friends; two extremely opposite personalities somehow enjoying each other's company. You made me laugh, and I introduced you to Deepak Chopra and Louise Hay. In return, you gave me some serious side eye and threw out some hippy-dippy comments. It was a time when you resisted personal growth because you were the girl who had a rough life but said you were "fine." The self-proclaimed high functioning human with a wall as long and high as that in China, from my perspective.

We ended up going through a lot together. Your crude humour and cut-the-bullshit attitude helped me stay sane in troubling waters. When I was dissolving my business partnership, and my anxiety was high, you were there to allow me to vent and helped me stand my ground. It was like a bad divorce and you one of the people who helped me to see the situation for what it was.

As time went on, you faced your own set of challenges. Your grandfather got sick with cancer and eventually passed away. Man, he was stubborn. But what I saw was how much he knew he could lean on you. When he reached his breaking point and fear set in, he would call you. I remember a phone call you took when we were out for dinner. He phoned you, uncertain of what to do and desperate for your help. Despite being shaken, you gathered yourself and found your way to him. You got him the care he needed and in the end, did the bravest thing of all by being with him during his final moments on earth.

Every relationship serves a purpose and brings lessons. People come to us precisely at a time we need them. They also leave in the same regard. A lot of years passed with us. Geez, some days it was like Cheech and Chong *minus the Mary Jane. Maybe even a little* Thelma and Louise. *Or* Driving Miss Daisy *with me as the damn driver. We had a lot of fun together. You came over to the hippy-dippy ways I embraced (your words, not mine), which was you choosing to be open-minded. I learned to lighten up and go with the flow. I also learned to deal with my annoyance when your ego came out strong. We shared a lot of experiences that would take pages upon pages to capture.*

One thing I know is that you enjoyed having people together from your dinner parties at your home to the FIERCE awards you created. Despite whatever you went through, you connected with others. That's always stood out to me, and even now I marvel at it as I watch you continue to make time for your family and friends.

That's a great trait, Plantass. Keep it.

Love,

Karissa

No one has the right to tell you how to process the death of a loved one. There is no set timeline for grief, no right amount of time to move on and no predetermined end date for the sadness no matter how many times you've lost someone.

My grandfather and I had a strange relationship. He gave me the name Tamara, was the only real father figure I had in my life and constantly challenged me to be better. I looked up to him when I was a kid but had no problem pushing back as an adult. We argued over the stupidest things: he was a Calgary Flames fan, and I loved the Edmonton Oilers, so our conversations became heated due to the rivalry between the two teams. When my grandma died, he insisted I go to college because that's what she would have wanted. When I got kicked out of college, I was terrified to tell him because of all the people in my life he was the only person in my life that I didn't want to disappoint. When I got a job as a sports writer at a daily paper, he asked what I was going to do next with my life.

He was there for every significant milestone, and when he became sick, I stopped everything I was doing and devoted my time to taking care of him.

I was with him when he found out he had cancer.

I helped him pick out a coffin.

I took him back and forth to the hospital.

I whispered that I would be OK and he could go.

I held his hand when he took his last breaths.

And I did it the way I did most things in my life. Alone.

He was the one person in my life I could always count on, and when he needed me the most, I was there because there was nowhere else I could be.

I may have felt alone when he was dying, but there were people around me who saw me go through it. I shared my journey online because writing about what I was experiencing was the only outlet I had to express how I felt and it became an online diary that I can look back on and see how far I've come. For three straight months, I put my life on hold to make sure that he wasn't alone as he took the final steps towards the end of his journey.

Karissa is absolutely to blame for pushing me onto this hippy-dippy path. She more, like, shoved me if I'm being completely honest here. Physically shoved me. Dragged me kicking and screaming into the spiritual realm, not gonna lie. She gave me two books for my birthday, *Seven Spiritual Laws of Success* by Deepak Chopra and *You Can Heal Your Life* by Louise Hay, a month before any of this shit happened with my grandpa, and ignored me when I rolled my eyes in disgust.

I had no idea those books would change everything for me, but before they did, I started pushing people away, Karissa included.

Being strong can break you, and once my grandpa died, that's what happened to me. I felt like I had been holding my breath for three months and started gasping for air after he died. It had been 17 years since my grandma passed away and I almost forgot how it felt to lose someone you loved.

I felt a tremendous sense of relief.

Then I felt guilty about feeling relieved.

I had the most intense, physical pain of absolute heartache because I missed him.

Then anger for leaving his life in a fucking mess for me to clean up.

And finally, I felt reluctance to face my life without him.

I didn't want to deal with his estate and all of the things that go along with that when someone dies. All I wanted to do was get through the funeral and not think about death or all the questions I wanted to ask him before he died but never did.

Staring at an empty chair across from me, I imagined him there and started asking those questions even though I didn't expect an answer.

Why didn't you take care of your shit while you were here to take care of it?

Why didn't you sell your own fucking house or tell me you were going to leave me as the executor of your estate?

Why did this blindside me?

What did grandma say before she died?

Why didn't you talk about her more?

Why can't this all just go away?

I broke down, collapsing in a heap on the floor and sobbed uncontrollably. "I can't do this," I said out loud. "I can't take care of this for you, and I can't go on as if nothing happened. I can't. I am not strong enough to do this," I screamed, looking at the empty chair, willing him to magically appear and answer the damn questions.

The tears finally stopped, and I laid there, mentally, emotionally and physically exhausted. Three months of watching someone you love, waste away like everything he had accomplished in his life meant nothing, took its toll.

And then the phone rang.

"Hello?"

It was his lawyer calling to check on me.

"I can't do this. I don't think I'm the person who should be taking care of this," I said, fighting to maintain my composure.

"Your grandfather wouldn't have chosen you to look after his estate if he didn't think you couldn't handle it. He believed in you and trusted you,' he said. "He knew you were strong enough to take care of this, but if you aren't able to do it, we can make alternative arrangements."

I looked at the empty chair and felt my grandpa smiling at me as if his lawyer addressed all of my concerns.

Seriously though, what lawyer calls just to check on someone?

"Tamara? Are you still there?"

I realized I had gone silent, looking at that chair and imagining my grandpa there.

"Uh, yeah, still here. I'll do it. I'll figure it out," I replied before thanking him and hanging up.

Of all the goodbyes I had said to people I loved, my grandfather's death forced me to change the most, and it wasn't for the better.

Over the course of the next couple of years, every conversation I had was laced with malice and cattiness. I wanted to fight all the time and started cutting people out of my life, left and right. I hated everything about almost everyone I came into contact with and refused to look at the source of my rage because that would mean seeing myself for who I had become and there was no way I wanted to do that. Instead, I looked for the worst in people and saw it. I hated myself, so I gravitated to other people who felt the same about themselves and fed off their energy. I'd flip between practicing the *Seven Spiritual Laws of Success* and engaging in the online drama of the day on social media.

Death can be
the greatest mindfuck of all time.

Death can change you even if you don't think you need to change. Death can make you examine who you are and who you don't want to be. Death can wrap you in its sinister embrace and squeeze the life out of you if you let it. Death can wake you up from a slumber you didn't even realize you were in. Death can make you forget how to love by making you believe the damage it leaves behind is irreparable. Death can convince you that pain is all you'll ever feel. Death is the most malicious liar and best teacher you'll ever have.

Hey Karissa,

Like most people during that time in my life, you knew me at my worst, but you could see something in me that few others did. You looked past the anger and the pain through to who I was yet, despite all the times you stood up for me, I eventually cut you out of my life just like everyone else.

I didn't even give you the courtesy of a message or anything. It was a dick move on my part, and I never apologized so let me say now that I'm sorry for doing that to you. You deserved better especially after all the times you defended me when you didn't have to.

Who I am now is partly because of who you are. You became a patch in this mosaic that I've rebuilt myself as so thank you for being a part of my life. As far as soulmates go, you're one I've kept tucked away in my not-so-inappropriate thoughts haha. We had some great times together and went through some shitty situations, too, but through it all, we could stay connected until I burned to the ground in, what I can only hope, has been my final phase of ascension. I wouldn't blame you if you were resentful or bitter but that isn't your nature so thank you for allowing me to become some part of your life again, even if it is only online.

Do you remember when we went to see that psychic, and we both had private sessions? She was telling me that there was someone I loved who stayed with me.

"I don't want to say it was a boyfriend but he was in your life, and there was love. His name started with a K. Do you know who it was?" she asked me. I remember catching my breath and immediately knowing it was Keon. Then she said there was a woman with him and her name started with an R, do you remember me telling you this? It was Keon's mom, Ruth. I knew then that she had passed away.

And remember that time you helped me clean out my grandpa's house after he died? I still get chills when I think about how I was on the other side of the basement sweeping, and you were in the furnace room vacuuming, and how I heard you yell, "MOTHERFUCKER!" I went over to see what was wrong but you thought it was me who swore. We were both confused, wondering who the hell could be in the house because it was only you and me cleaning. In between where I was sweeping and the furnace room (fuck, I'm getting chills again) there was cold storage space. It was like some fucking spirit was trapped there. I remember going back to sweep but coming to see you again to ask you something. Before I went back to my chore, you asked me to plug the vacuum in again.

"What are you talking about?" I asked.

"Well it's turned off so didn't you unplug it to talk to me?" you replied.

"No, why the hell would I do that?"

Remember the look on our faces when we saw that the vacuum cord was, indeed, unplugged? That was it for both of us lol we ran out of that house. Anyway, thanks for being you. You were a course-correction soulmate for me, and I'm grateful you came into my life.

As the hippy-dippies say, love and light my friend.

Love,

t.

The Lessons:

Hitting rock bottom can be the greatest gift you're blessed with in this lifetime. You have the power to decide who you want to be when you get back up again. You decide which version of you stays and which version of you gets buried along with your past.

Death brings about the end of a relationship, and those relationships are irreplaceable, but that doesn't mean you can't love again. You'll never lose the same person twice: sibling, parent, grandparent, child, friend, mentor or lover. Every connection is different and how you feel when they pass away is never the same as when another relationship ends.

Believe what you want

If you need to go to a church or mosque or a graveyard

to honour a loved one, then you should do it. But don't impose those beliefs onto someone else who is looking for answers.

If following what you've learned doesn't suit your belief system, but you aren't sure what you want to believe in, be open to other religions and philosophies. Take what you need and discard what doesn't match your vibe. I knew I had a relationship with angels so I started exploring and discovered I could tap into messages through angel tarot cards.

I also found myself drawn to other Gods and Goddesses, not by reading a bible or studying other religions but by being open to signs placed in my path. The summer after my grandfather's death, I was at a festival and walked past a pop-up shop that showcased leather-bound journals. I looked at the covers and settled on a leather-bound book with an etched elephant. Not knowing what it was, and believing elephants were a sign of good luck, I was captivated by the design and fascinated by the image. The vendor watched me pick up the book and run my fingers over the artwork, trying to figure out what it was when he said, "Lord Ganesha protects you."

"Who?"

"Lord Ganesha is the remover of obstacles and provider of abundance," he responded.

"I have no idea who he is, but I love that concept!"

He smiled at me as I handed him the money and wandered off with my purchase. When I got home, I

Googled Lord Ganesha and was amazed at what I found. Lord Ganesha is a Hindu God who represents generosity, protection, and prosperity. He is known for clearing the path for those who ask and helping them through their journey. He was the spiritual figure I needed in my life and I was grateful that he came into my path. I've always been drawn to the symbolism of angel numbers and spirit animals, and look for meaning beyond the surface of what's presented as coincidence. His presence at that time in my life was no coincidence.

It was around this time that I stumbled across the Japanese legend of the Red String of Fate. The story says that two people connected by this thread will have moments that shape their path and will meet each lifetime, regardless of the time, place or circumstances. These two souls have something to learn from each other and will come into your life when you need them the most in the form of parents, siblings, children, friends or strangers you meet at "random." (There's no such thing as random or coincidence, it's all part of divine timing and universal energy). The red string might get tangled, knotted or stretched which means they will meet other people along the way or choose a path that will take them away from the other person, but it does not break.

Keon's death led me to experience the loss of what I now understand to be a soulmate because it was based on romantic love. In Grade 5, I had read about the Greek philosopher Plato's *Symposium* which started the whole soulmate/twin flame ideology. He wrote that humans were originally two souls in one body with four arms, four legs and a head with two faces. Zeus, the God of all Olympian Gods, feared the powerful humans because they were threatening to take over Mt. Olympus, so he split their bodies in half. As if that weren't enough, he condemned them to spend their lives searching for their other half; ergo the soulmate theory was born.

As a kid, I liked the idea that there was only one special person out there for me. It was romantic but not my reality which is why I fell in love with the Red String of Fate. Not only did it make sense that a soulmate was someone you loved who you didn't have to be "in love" with but it opened up a whole new world of possibilities for romantic love. You can fall in love multiple times throughout your life instead of being tied to your "one and only" forever. What if you break up with your soulmate when you're 16? Are you destined to settle for lame-ass connections that have no deeper meaning than, "Meh, you'll do," or is it possible that when your connection ends, another one will come into your life?

AHA!

Exactly!

My grandfather's death opened my eyes to the world around me through searching for answers about how we're all connected and gave me the opportunity to look outside of my limited beliefs for what my soul needed to remember. Maybe it's because he fought for me to have the chance to study Islam when we lived in Kuwait and told me to respect other people's beliefs. Or perhaps it's because Karissa reminded me to be open to reading about ideas I'd never heard of before when she gave me those books.

Whatever it was, being open to other faiths and finding the fit with what I needed at that time has served me well by not forcing myself into a box designed to keep people out. When you have no restrictions on what you're willing to listen to, you are more likely to find what you need.

A belief system doesn't have to be one you're born into or handed as you blindly accept; it can be something you create for yourself by opening your eyes to the world around you. I'm a student of the universe and will continue to learn and accept what resonates with my soul.

My greatest salvation came in the form of an event I created to recognize others called the FIERCE awards. I developed the project in 2009 to celebrate people who make a difference whether it was in their own life or the lives of others. Finding purpose in death gives you a reason to continue regardless of the scale of the lives you touch.

I didn't start out with the intention of helping people or validating others through the awards but that's exactly what happened. More importantly, the event became like a glorious balloon of hope that I held onto as it soared year after year, as I recovered through that moment in my life. At the end of the 5-year run, I had shared the stories of 212 men and women across Alberta, and healed the wounds of my past. Could I have done that if I hadn't experienced the life I had to that point? Maybe. But my journey allowed me to appreciate the sacrifices others made daily to improve the lives of those around them, and go through my healing journey by exchanging pain for purpose.

I reached out to my friend, Molly McCord, who is an intuitive psychic healer, author, and spiritual business coach, for advice on how to heal the pain of my past.

"Forgiveness is your life purpose," she said.

I laughed out loud and replied, "I'm a Scorpio, Molly. You should know that we don't forgive and we sure as fuck don't forget."

"You have free will and don't have to believe it but I feel like forgiveness is part of what you need to heal in this lifetime."

"Uh huh," I replied, thinking she had her woo-woo wires crossed on that divine message but I filed that away for another time and thanked her for the insight.

Tim McLean

I have a tough time reading the news especially when some tragedy is front and centre on social media. It's part of being an empath, someone who automatically feels the pain others are going through and takes on the energy of what they're feeling. I don't attach myself to a tragedy to be a part of it or need to insert myself into the pain by connecting it back to me because it has nothing to do with me. I feel genuinely for others, and when something happens to someone I've never met, but their story is all over the news, I want to help them through it. It becomes a physical pain, one I can feel in my heart and consumes my energy. I've learned to surround myself with significant boundaries to shelter myself from absorbing other people's emotions and stay away from the news I know will cause this intense sorrow.

The only time I reached out to someone I'd never met was after reading about the horrific murder of Tim McLean, the young man who was savagely killed on a Greyhound bus, July 30, 2008, 30 km west of Portage la Prairie, Manitoba. I was a young mom who couldn't imagine the pain his mom was dealing with upon learning the details of her son's death. I didn't know her, but my heart broke into a thousand pieces for her as the details of Timothy's death made headlines across the world.

Stabbed.
Torn apart.
Cannibalized.
Decapitated.

Horrified passengers scrambled to try and help but couldn't stop the carnage. They escaped off the bus and watched the scene unfold, blocking the door so his murderer couldn't escape. Vince Li, who had untreated Schizophrenia, was found Not Criminally Responsible and spent seven years at Selkirk Mental Health Centre before moving to Winnipeg to be treated at the Health Science Centre as an outpatient. Li was released with a new identity and no criminal record in February 2017.

When I sent an email to Carol de Delley asking if I could interview her for a magazine I published, I didn't expect a reply. I wanted to share the story from her perspective and let her know how sorry I was for the pain she was suffering. We were in different provinces, and there was no reason she needed to respond to my request almost a year after Timothy's murder, but she did, and we set up an interview.

To that point in my career, I'd steered away from news due to the sensitive nature and prying into people's pain that was required to write their stories. There was no reason for me, at that point, to change directions but I was compelled to share her story. When she called, I could barely bring myself to ask any questions. Instead, I listened as she told me the details of what happened and her initial reaction to the news.

"I saw the news on TV, and my first thought was that I felt awful for that poor young man's family," she said. "I had no idea it was Timothy."

She sent me photos of Timothy to use for the article, simple moments from his life that showcased his charming grin and the mischievous look in his eyes. I looked at the photos from the time he was a baby until before his death at 22 years old and felt unbelievably connected to both Timothy and Carol. Nothing I could do or say would help her or make a difference in her life, but I promised to share his story as much as possible as she began her fight to have the NCR law changed.

When I was writing the article, my computer would suddenly freeze or shut off, and sometimes I'd end up falling into my chair because it was set to the lowest point even though it wasn't like that when I got up from it. I began to wonder about Timothy because it felt like he was hanging around while I wrote the story to make sure I got it right. I emailed Carol and asked if he liked to play pranks on people. She replied that his nickname was the JoKaWild and that it probably was him messing with my stuff. After all the experiences I'd had with spirits, I wasn't surprised so I kindly asked Timothy to knock it off with my computer because I couldn't risk losing my article. After that, it stopped. Spirits are good like that; they listen when you tell them something.

Carol achieved a small victory in her efforts, and Bill C-54 passed in 2013 with updates to the NCR law which include waiting three years for a review instead of one, making public safety the "paramount" consideration for review boards and notify victims when a "high-risk" offender is released.

I've stayed in touch with Carol over the years, and we've had dinner a couple of times talking about everything from Timothy to her fight to change the NCR law to challenges we've both faced. Her strength astounds me, and she has survived more over the past ten years than anyone should have to go through in one lifetime. Her story is hers to tell, and I'm looking forward to the day she writes it because no one can do a book justice except for her.

Pain is always attached to death, but when it comes in the form of a heinous crime, there's another level of rage that you can't understand unless you go through it. Timothy's death affected his family differently than it impacted the people on that Greyhound Bus and yet another way that it touched the lives of the first responders and RCMP. As a result of PTSD, Corporal Ken Barker of the RCMP who was one of the first on the scene, committed suicide almost six years to the day of Timothy's murder.

Carol told me that Tim was her wild child.

"He was a rebel and lived his life to the fullest. Always. He would say to me, 'I'm gonna be famous one day, mom! I'm gonna be famous!'

"I never imagined it would be for his last day here."

5

Cue the woo-woo train

Dear Tamara,

Being friends with you from 18-22 was an important part of my life and had a significant impact on who I am today.

I always felt we were kindred spirits. We seemed to get each other when no one else understood what we were thinking or doing or needing.

I remember you as brazen and independent, fierce, strong and guarded at times but always loyal and always with a big heart.

I think that's what drew me to you the most; when you were making a difference, you didn't even realize it. You were yourself. When you tried to be that way, it was different and didn't have the same effect. When you were yourself, without the effort, you had this beautiful aura about you.

Do you remember your 21st birthday when we went to the Cromdale Hotel for a drink with your mom? You were excited and proud because you were going back to your roots in the inner city, and yet a part of you was guarded because of the hotel's reputation. It was rough, seedy and some sketchy people frequented the establishment, but you knew how important it would be for your mom to stop in and toast her on her 39th birthday. You were doing something for your mom that didn't require a lot of effort but it made her feel like she mattered and that she was loved. I could tell by your mom's smile that it meant a lot to her.

It is one of my favourite memories of you and your mom because I know how much you struggled with that relationship.

You don't see the imprint you leave on someone's life, Tamara. I wish you could see that for yourself.

I've never had a connection with anyone the way we are connected as soul sisters. I believe that with my heart. Despite ups & downs, fights, long distance, life getting in the way and changes we've both gone through, our friendship has lasted the test of time.

Nothing can break our bond; it can be stretched sometimes but never broken.

My biggest fear when we were younger was your mood swings. Your mood could switch at the snap of your fingers. It seemed to get worse as we got older through those years. You would make plans for us to get together and about two hours into our night out would decide you'd had enough and wanted to go home. No warning, no idea why the sudden change of heart, you were just done. It was very frustrating when it happened because I didn't want to go home. It was even more aggravating because I often I drove an hour from out of town, picked you up and drove us wherever we needed to go. I couldn't just tell you to leave when you acted that way because I had to drive you back home and my night ended up being over, too. I never knew what would set you off, you never told me. Maybe something happened, or someone said something or you saw someone who upset you. I never knew, but it came on suddenly and just like that; no changing your mind.

Planning nights out with you was tough because there was always a concern that you would go from happy to angry for no apparent reason.

You know what I loved most about you, though? There was never any judgement from you about my behaviour or actions or what I had to say. I could be

119

myself, and I think you had the same effect on all your friends. I know your relationship with your mom was a big reason you were so close with your friends; it's like you chose your family because your family life wasn't great. Your friends seemed to mean more to you than your relatives especially after your grandma passed away.

I remember visiting your grandma's younger sister with you after you lost your grandma. You went because you thought your grandma would have wanted you to keep in touch with the family. You were like that; you did things out of respect for your grandma despite how you felt about your family. It was important to you to honour her, and I always respected how close you were to your grandma and how even after death you carried on that tradition of respect.

It's too bad you didn't have that same relationship with your mom, but I understand why you felt the way you did. You never wanted to be like your mom, and you did everything to make sure you didn't end up like her. It's funny how things come full circle because if I look back at who we were when we were at that time in our lives to who we have become, neither of us would have expected our lives to turn out the way they have. Now you have a beautiful daughter who you share an amazing bond with and have even developed a strong connection with my daughter.

Everything has come full circle for you, Tamara. Karma, angels, destiny; I don't know if anyone else believes in it, but because of you, I know it exists.

Love,

Teresa

Ugh.

Gross.

Teresa had always had a sappy way of expressing her feelings and back then when we were going to the nightclubs and sowing the wildest of oats, we would have the most profound conversations about life, love and what the future would bring. She gave me heartfelt cards with long, handwritten notes expressing her undying friendship and love, saying we were connected as soul sisters forever. I thought there was something inherently wrong with her like her brain was wired with unicorn sparkles and flowery prose because she made me want to throw up in my mouth whenever she got in one of her sentimental moods. It weirded me out back then. She was the only person in my life to ever communicate with me like that. She forced me to look beyond the surface of a situation and uncover truths about myself that I preferred to ignore.

I loved her more than I loved anyone in my life at that time. She's the only person who has seen me go through this journey, almost from the beginning, and she's stayed in my life regardless of distance or time. Friendships like the one I have with Teresa are rare; she talked me off the ledge more times than she remembers, and has been a part of some of the most significant moments in my life.

When my grandma died, I wanted to hide under the blankets and stay in my apartment, refusing to talk to anyone. She came over and practically dragged me out to Klondike Days, the annual travelling fair in Edmonton, and wouldn't let me feel sorry for myself. I hated her at the time, thinking she had no idea what I was going through, but her intentions were for all the right reasons.

I moved away to start my career, and she moved away to have a baby. Our years of partying had come to a natural end as we both grew up and began new chapters in our lives. We stayed connected, but it wasn't as easy as it is now. There was no texting or Facebook or Skype or anything other than phone calls and letters (we weren't far off from horse and buggy if I'm honest here), but we managed to keep in touch.

Teresa knew my relationship with my mom was bad, but even she didn't understand the depths of anger I held for my mother. She didn't know the reason my mood swings went from 0 to 1000 in the blink of an eye was the suppressed rage I had for the abuse I endured as a kid and the blame I placed on my mom because of it. Those memories would come rushing back, triggered in a movie theatre watching *Sleepers*. It's a story about four boys from Hell's Kitchen who suffer extreme abuse at the hands of the guards. One scene where the boys quietly walk down a dimly lit hallway knowing what's about to happen as the guards walked behind them, cracked open the crypt where I had buried the demons from my past. I left the theatre shaking and almost doubled over from the recollections that were forcing their way into my consciousness. From that moment on, I started to remember the details of my abuse and my relationship with my mom went from terrible to irreparable.

I questioned her reasons for making the choices she made in her life that led her down a path of self-destruction, causing the people around her to suffer. The more self-pity she had, the more resentment I had towards her. She was the victim in her story and refused to make changes that would give her a chance at a better life. And I hated her for it.

It took years of painful interactions but eventually, I cut my mom out of my life, refusing to allow her toxicity to envelope me because it was affecting the people I loved by bringing out the worst in who I had become. And I had become pretty fuckin' dark.

"Tamara, call me. It's about your mom."

I looked at the text and my heart sank. I instinctively knew what had happened.

"Why?" I texted back.

"She died yesterday. Just thought you should know."

"Fuck," I muttered to myself. "Of course she did."

Dear Mom,

Remember that time when you were in the hospital in the ICU because of kidney failure? I reluctantly dropped everything I was doing to drive out to the hospital to see you, not because I wanted to see you but because, like always, I had to take care of things for you. I was busy doing life purpose shit when I got the call from Travis' mom who said you were basically on your deathbed and that I "owed it to you" to see you "just in case."

I didn't owe you shit, I told her.

Cold, right? She gave me shit for being so ungrateful, and I get now that she only knew me from what you told her, which probably wasn't very nice, but she didn't know the full story of our relationship.

Sure, I guess looking from the outside into our relationship, from anyone else's perspective who didn't know me or the reasons why I chose to cut you out of my life, yeah, I was a bitch. But I was the bitch who had to clean up your mess time and time again since I was a kid. I don't remember many moments of you being a mom, but I knew that I couldn't let you die alone. So I drove to the hospital with only one thought in my mind: please don't die.

There were selfish reasons that I didn't want you to die, and I suddenly felt that little girl inside of me who didn't want to lose her mom.

"Please don't die," I repeated over and over and over to myself.

The angels must have heard me because, by some miracle, you pulled through even though the nurse told me not to expect anything. I was grateful and resentful and hated everything about the conversation we had after you got out of the hospital. You knew I was mad about having to come to the hospital, but you didn't know how much the idea of you dying broke my heart. You told me that when you died, you didn't want me at your funeral, so I replied that I didn't care because, at that moment, I didn't.

Less than five months later, you died on your 57th birthday. Heart attack. You were the same age as grandma was when she died.

We hadn't spoken since that call, and I remember sitting at my kitchen table, processing the news and remembering all the deaths that had lead up to that moment. Uncle Darrell, grandma, Keon, grandpa and now you. I wasn't sad that you died; I was sad that you never lived while you had the chance.

You were there with me. I felt your presence and looked towards you, knowing you were standing there, looking at me. We had the best conversation. You came to me because you couldn't move on until I forgave you for all the mistakes you made in your life that impacted mine. At that moment, I released every ounce of anger, pain, resentment, and sadness I had for you.

And then you told me that I needed to forgive myself. It was as though every word between us had led to that moment in my life, and I walked straight into the light at the end of the tunnel. That was the key to how I went from abrasive and toxic to this ascension of inner peace.

I never got to say thank you for being my mom or the making the choices you did because they shaped who I am now. Without everything you went through, I wouldn't be the person I am today.

I love you, mom.

t.

The Lessons:

Well, look at that, Molly was right! Forgiveness was part of my life purpose and it took my mom's death to figure that one out.

Not every person who comes into your life has to stay regardless of the relationship. Family dynamics can be the trickiest to navigate because there is a sense of obligation to stay connected to relatives.

You

are

not

obligated

to keep

anyone

in your life.

Not your mom, not your dad, not your siblings, not one person is entitled to a spot at your table. It doesn't matter who they are or what their relationship is to you; if they bring out the worst in you or hold you to your past mistakes or continually project their issues onto you, let them go.

What can you learn from soulmates like these?

Who do you want to be? People who come into your life that bring toxic energy or drama or inflict pain are there to show you who you are and how resilient you can be. Soulmates can be placed temporarily on your path and return for a more profound soul lesson that will catapult you to another ascension of your highest self.

Cue the woo-woo train.

These soulmates are your best teachers because they force you to dig deep and uncover the core of who you are. You are made of the universe and come from the stars, and sometimes you need the reminder which is why different soulmates in your life. Some are mirrors of your inner self and reflect the chaos inside of you; some are healers who help you understand the lessons and allow you to grow through the pain, while others are in your life to show you who you can be. When you figure out the reason these soulmates have made an appearance, you rarely see them again in any form. Sometimes it takes multiple adaptations of the same soulmate to come into your life before you see the bigger picture and learn the lessons. Here's the tricky part: you might think you've been there, done that but if you only breeze through the class without real comprehension of the lesson, you will have to take summer school.

Or a course upgrade.

Or advanced education.

You will keep stumbling upon the same soulmates until one day that lightbulb goes off and YOU FINALLY GET IT!

Lesson learned, now what?

It's important to sever cords of attachment to people who no longer serve your greatest and highest good. Wait. You know what? Fuck that. I hate that phrase, "serve your greatest and highest good." It's a spiritual term that has been floating around forever, and the more I think about it, the more it annoys me (excuse me while I go off on this little tangent). The interpretation of the word "serve" can be defined as being there to cater to your needs. That's not the case when it comes to soulmates.

Soulmates play a vital role in your ascension. They are there to guide, teach and reflect who you are. The notion that someone comes into your life to serve you makes it sound like you are the centre of their universe. You are not. We are all connected and here to teach each other through our interactions and relationships. So, the idea of cutting people out of your life because they no longer "serve" a purpose sounds entitled and selfish which

I know you're not.

However.

It is essential to cut the energetic cords to anyone who brings lousy juju your way.

You are a magnet for awesome! Remember that! And your soulmates will reflect that inner beauty, my friend.

Inner peace like a beast!

Cutting people out of my life has never been difficult for me. I tend to look at bad relationships like a tumour so if I find myself connected to someone who brings out some of my darker tendencies I will remove myself from their life. Ending relationships can be challenging if they are unwilling to let go of you. I've experienced it on both sides, clinging to bad friendships because I was afraid of being alone or having someone like my mom (the woman gave birth to me) who stayed energetically connected even though I didn't see her much. I'm fortunate because her death brought us closer together through understanding forgiveness.

It's amazing what you can learn from death once you sift through the emotional trauma.

How do you forgive?

Forgiveness is a tricky word.

To some, it conjures up images of condoning someone's actions or offering absolution. To others, it's a way of healing the past and putting it behind them.

The context of the word "forgive" is crucial when deciding whether or not you want to use it in the circumstance that you're applying it.

"Don't worry about it, don't sweat it, no big deal, all good, forget about it..."

But to have to offer forgiveness to someone who has caused grief, pain, sadness, or worse?

That can leave you wondering why you are the one who is left to forgive when they are the one who inflicted pain.

Healing starts with you, and you are the only person who can begin that process. No one else can forgive yourself or someone else for you or let go of the trauma you've endured. The scales of justice are unbalanced in this scenario, I get it, but if you are the one left carrying the burden of resentment and the weight of memories, you are the only one who can release it.

When something happens to you or around you, the natural reaction is to look for the culprit so they can bear the brunt of the blame. You want to lash out, you want revenge, you want them to feel the same pain they've caused you because then you will feel some sense of relief.

Unfortunately, it doesn't work that way.

Some people need to hear that you forgive them so they can make peace with their actions and move on with their lives. Others want you to forgive them so that you're saying, "Hey, it's OK that you treated me like that!" When they treat you like that again, they'll ask for your forgiveness again, expecting the same response. Vicious cycle.

You have to determine if you're ready to forgive and let go or if you don't care enough about that person to offer forgiveness.

Most of the time, for me, it's the latter. I can shut my feelings off about someone LIKE THAT, no thought required. They don't need my forgiveness; they need to get the hell outta my life and stay out.

But I get it; some people need to forgive someone who has caused them harm or pain so that they can move on. They need to use the word because it helps them heal. It's a complicated emotion that requires an individual application to individual circumstances.

For example, when my mom was alive, I was never able to "forgive her" for the past. I merely decided to use my history as a lesson in how not to live my future. It worked for me right up until she died. Only then did I feel that she needed me to forgive her so that her spirit could move on. Now if you're not spiritual or believe in past lives, you'll think that's a crock of shit, but for me, it was my reality.

My soul sighed out of relief when I said, "I forgive

you," to my mom and ultimately forgave myself.

If I need to forgive someone who has hurt me, it means that I am attached to that pain or that person when in reality, I go full Samurai on those ties more effortlessly than most people do. Indifference is my ultimate release. It allows me to cut attachments to people and any hurt they may have caused. Is it forgiveness? Sure, why not. I've come to accept that it's my second favourite F-word.

To attach an emotion to something or someone is draining especially when that emotion is painful or anger or resentment.

How do you forgive someone who's caused you trauma or changed your life by their actions?

Compassion?

Understanding?

Love???

That would be a big ol' fuck no.

I detached and reclaimed my power by not allowing them the benefit of being connected to me by forgiving myself, healing my feelings, and purging them from my life. I won't share energetic cords if I don't give them a way to BE connected to me.

In the end, I believed, forgiveness was merely a word until I understood that forgiveness wasn't about them, it was about me.

Saying goodbye to a Graceful Goddess

July 10, 2012

I've been dreading the fact that I had to write this post since I heard the news last night.

There is a woman who most of you have never heard of before. She lived a happy, quiet, and full life, generously touching the lives of others with her kindness and inner peace. She glowed from the inside out, her warmth and soothing presence calming the inconsolable, and her first thought was always of how she could help someone in need.

Christine Jarvis was the first-ever Graceful Goddess recipient of the FIERCE Awards but more than that, she was someone I considered a friend.

On Saturday, July 7, 2012, Christine died doing one of the things she loved most; driving her cherished motorcycle that she lovingly named Rosie. I couldn't stop crying when I heard the news, thinking of how much light she spread to those around her. It didn't seem fair to lose such a beautiful soul at such a young age.

At the 2011 FIERCE awards, I invited the previous winners to present awards and Chris graciously accepted the offer. During her speech, she spoke of how much it meant to her to have the honour of being our first-ever Graceful Goddess recipient and how she looked at her diamond award whenever she needed a reminder that she was FIERCE.

Chris was 51 years old when she died, but she touched so many lives in her short time here. She leaves behind three children, three grandchildren and countless lives she has changed for the better.

Rest in peace, graceful goddess. The world is a better place because you were here.

t.

6

Don't wait for death to be the wakeup call you need to live your life

---

Hey Tamara,

Our friendship started because of the love we shared for one man, my husband Travis who was also your childhood friend and childhood crush (don't deny it, everyone knows it's true!). I had always heard about this "Tamara" from his mom, your mom's best friend because you had the biggest crush on Travis when you guys were growing up. I would laugh at the stories they told me and wanted to meet you to let you know Travis was my man haha.

Back then Travis and I had started our family by the time I got to meet you. You were not at all what I expected. I liked you!!! We hit it off right away. You would come over, and we would sit for hours drinking coffee. You were a bit of a wild child who liked to party and have fun whereas I was in "mom" mode. We were at very different stages of our lives, but our friendship still seemed to work. Then one day you came to tell us you were moving away for work. Travis and I couldn't believe it, but we were so proud of you. And just like that, you were gone, and we never heard from you in forever, it seemed.

Over the next few years, we never saw you much, but occasionally I would reach out to you to see how you were doing and catch up. Travis always thought of you as his little sister, and I knew he would never be the one to reach out to you, it wasn't his style, so I did it for him. I knew it was important to Travis that he always knew that you were OK. He thanked me for keeping in touch with you over the years because he knew I would find a way to get a hold of you when I needed to.

When Travis' mom passed away, I asked him if he wanted me to get a hold of you so he could tell you and, of course, he said yes. It had been years since we spoke last, so I had no idea where to begin looking for you. I found your website and sent an email telling you that Travis wanted to talk to you. I gave you his number, and you called him right away. He was so happy to hear from you despite the circumstances. We met you shortly after that for dinner, and our friendship blossomed once again.

We had just over a year of getting together again and making plans to travel together before my world came crashing down around me. The man who meant everything to me was taken away with no warning. Travis had a massive heart attack at only 44 years old. Just like that, he was gone.

I knew I had to phone you. Honestly, I don't remember much of what I said when I left a message for you in the middle of the night or what I said when you called me back a few hours later. Everything is pretty much a blur to me. I just know that since that moment, anytime I needed advice or someone to chat with or a hug, I could always count on you. The man who brought us together when he was alive brought us even closer with his death. Even though you were Travis' friend first, I knew that I could say anything to you or ask you anything and you would never judge me. When I don't understand how I'm feeling or even things that my kids are going through, you are the one that I can turn to for advice. I love how you look at things so spiritually and how you explained soulmates to me, how everyone comes into your life for a reason. We're all connected in some way, you said, and soulmates aren't only husband and wife relationships but can be friendships, too. Travis was both our soulmates, different types for each of us but still soulmates. I am grateful he brought you into my life.

You are stuck with me forever, Tamara.

No tears, only love.

Love you forever and ever,

Karen

Nothing good can ever come from a text at 1 a.m. that reads, "Call me as soon as you wake up, it doesn't matter what time it is."

I woke up at 5 a.m, on the second day of a new job, and knew exactly what the text meant the minute I saw it. Knowing didn't make it any easier to hear the words.

"Hi, Tamara."

"What happened?"

"He died," she said, fighting back the tears.

I caught my breath and slumped over the counter, holding the phone to my ear.

"What? What happened?!! Are you OK? Fuck, of course you're not. Have you slept? Where are the kids?"

I had a million questions and wanted to take away some of the burdens of what she was about to go through.

I hope this wasn't his way of getting out of our plans for next week, I thought, feeling myself start to break. "Anything you need, I'm here," I told her, composing myself. "You'll need to make arrangements and start getting things in order, but I will help you. Let me help. I don't want you to go through this alone."

Karen only leaned on me a couple of times and stood in her power throughout the next few days, making sure she was there for her kids. She carried the pain with her but didn't let it show. I stayed close for the next few months, letting her know I was there whenever she needed me. She lost a husband, her best friend, the father of her children and I couldn't imagine the grief she carried. No death I had been through could help me console or empathize with what she was going through, so I just listened without offering advice.

Travis was more family to me than any relative I had that was still alive. I'd known and loved him since I was five years old, not in a romantic way other than the crush I had on him when we were kids, but in the way you love someone and can't imagine your life without them. We grew up together in the inner city, and our moms were best friends. Trav and I loved sharing stories of growing up in a world where few made it out, and we admired each other's strength and courage for moving away and building a life outside of the inner city.

I remember when Karen sent that email, telling me to call Travis. It was a couple of months after *Forgiveness and Other Stupid Things* came out, and all I could think of was that he had read the book and was pissed at me for mentioning the relationship between our moms. He was the older brother I never had and the idea that he was going to give me shit bothered me, even though I hadn't talked to him in a couple of years.

"Hey Travis, how are you?"

"Hey Tamara, I'm not doing so good. Mom passed, and I thought you would want to know."

"Fuck, I am so sorry to hear that! Are you OK? Ugh, of course you're not. What happened?"

Cancer claimed yet another loved one, and although I was not close to his mom, I felt terrible for Travis because, unlike me, he had a good relationship with his mom.

Her death reconnected us, and I got to spend the next 16 months in his life until death selfishly took him away from everyone he loved.

Travis was a soulmate, and I felt like every loss I had experienced to that point prepared me for what I needed to learn next. Before I could do that, I had to understand that soulmates come into our lives at the most critical times and comprehending the "why" can help process the grief you feel when they leave.

Hey Travis,

It's been almost a year since I saw you.

It was your 44th birthday, and if I had known it was the last time I would ever get to hug you, I wouldn't have left.

I know I have this stupid thing about capturing moments through photos whenever I'm with someone, but I don't regret it because I have the selfie of you and me from that night. Just like always, you put up with my demand for a photo, and I kissed your cheek, telling you I loved you.

That was the last thing I ever said to you,

and you said you loved me too. I've kept that with me this past year, thinking how fortunate I am to have that be our last interaction. There is no room for regret, only love.

Before I moved to Kelowna, you and Karen had me over to celebrate my new chapter. You were supportive in every way but do you remember how you insisted that I not become too stuck up when I became "successful."

I rolled my eyes and told you to shut up, but you said, "Just don't be a snob. I won't put up with that."

I hugged you and said, "Whatever, jackass. I love you. See you guys in a few months."

Months turned into years but Karen reached out after your mom died, which was only a couple of months after I published Forgiveness and Other Stupid Things, and I remember thinking, "Ah, fuck, Trav is going to give me shit for writing about his mom's friendship with my mom." I didn't want to call you. In fact, I avoided it, thinking that I could pretend I never got the email, but my conscience wouldn't let me get through the day without calling. Not gonna lie, a part of me was relieved that you weren't mad at me, but I felt terrible that you had to go through the process of watching your mom die. Another part of me was touched that you would even think of me during that time in your life, but it validated the idea that we were connected on a level that goes deeper than friendship. I don't care that family wasn't the tie that bonded us, you were the brother I never had, and I know you felt the same way about me. When you texted me the night of your birthday and said I was the sister you always wanted, I teared up.

Fucker. I hate getting emotional, and you know it, but I'll blame it on the wine, and you can blame it on the Jagermeister *puke*.

Despite all that I know about death, I hate the fact that you're not here. Some days, it doesn't seem real. Time is like that, I guess. It was like that when we hadn't seen each other in years, and it's like that now; moments turn into years, but you're still gone.

Not to get mushy or whatever but I love you, Travis. I always have and I always will. Catch you in the next lifetime, my brother.

Love,

t.

The Lessons:

Don't fucking ask someone who just lost a person they love if they're OK. They're not OK. It's a natural response, and I've done it more times than I can count but it's a dumb thing to say.

Try this:

"I'm listening," and then do it without interjecting to tell your own story about experiences you've had.

Don't ask for the details

When someone dies, it's human nature to want to know how it happened but to the person who is grieving, they are reliving it every single time you ask them about it.

Ask yourself:

Why did they come into my life?

What did they need to teach me?

What's my before and after? Who was I before I met them and who am I now since they've left?

How were they connected to the other people around me and why were they in their lives?

What kind of soulmate were they?

Diving into these questions can help with the grieving process by uncovering the reasons they were in your life. Understanding why a soulmate comes into your life doesn't eliminate grief, but it helps compartmentalize the relationship and eventually brings you to the point where you're emotionally ready to move forward without guilt.

When a soul connection permanently leaves this lifetime, it's because their physical journey is complete, fair or not. The love you bring into this lifetime doesn't end with death; the energy is infinite.

People die, but soulmates stay connected, lifetime after lifetime, and when you reconnect, they're not always the same type of soulmate they were in this lifetime. They might come back into your life as a mentor instead of a friend or a parent instead of a healer. Recognizing soulmates is the key to soul growth and ascension which is why it's important to know why they come into your life and how you can accelerate the lessons without losing the connection.

Every death has forced me to go within to understand what it means and how death is connected to life and **this is what I discovered with Travis' passing:**

Life unfolds the way it's supposed to and the people who come into our life bring something that we need to know. It's up to us whether we learn the lesson or not. You can carry on the way you have been living up to that point but maybe it takes them being ripped out of your life to understand what you were supposed to learn. It shouldn't be that way.

You shouldn't have to lose someone to learn what you needed to know but sometimes it's the only way you get to to move forward with your life. The problem is that we usually see loss and death as a punishment instead of the blessing that it truly is. Why are you losing someone? What were you supposed to learn? Have you learned the lesson? Do you understand how you're supposed to move forward?

Most people end up stuck in the why and moving on with their life even though time never really stops; it's just an illusion. Time keeps ticking away and life goes on with or without that person physically being there but most times, we get trapped in this moment of grief where you are paralyzed by it. Nothing makes sense, not the death, not the reason, not the lesson and definitely not the loss. But you can't change it. Death is absolute, for this moment anyway, and the trick is to keep moving through space and time to continue your journey while figuring out what you needed to learn.

You are constantly evolving into the brightest ascension of your being. Death pushes you further along the path, reminding you of your purpose and nudging you back onto the path you're meant to be on.

Yes, it fucking sucks that they're no longer with you in the physical realm but they will always be with you in spirit and that's what you need to tap into in order to maintain a connection. With loss comes the inevitable emotions of denial and anger, and you examine everything from your last conversation to wondering what the final moments were like for that person.

I know they're dead but I want them here.

It isn't fair.

This doesn't make sense.

Why did he have to die when there are so many other people who should have gone instead?

Why am I left here to live when they have to die?

It would have been better if it had been me because at least then I wouldn't have to deal with the pain.

Having someone suddenly removed from your life by death raises a thousand questions and brings a tornado of emotions from anger to denial to negotiation to shock to devastation and everything else in between. There's no room for acceptance until you've allowed everything else to consume you and then, only then, can you begin to heal from death. The only person who can get you through it is you. It's like losing weight: you can buy all the gym memberships you want, hire all the trainers, read all the books and say you'll lose weight but unless you do the work yourself, that weight ain't comin' off. Getting through grief is like that. Knowing the stages of grief, getting help from a counsellor and leaning on people you love during your darkest moments will only get you so far. You'll go through it on your own schedule but the healing has to happen from the inside out and only you can do that.

Grief isn't new to this world;
it's new to you.

Other people have suffered similar loss and made it through; you will, too. How you get there is up to you but make no mistake, you are not alone in this journey regardless of how isolated you might feel.

Death hasn't touched you alone; it has ripple effects of the relationship surrounding the person who died. Your relationship to them is unique and how you process the grief will be different than the casual acquaintance who lost the same person. As overwhelming as it might be, you are not the only person who is suffering from the loss. Being connected as soulmates gives everyone the same allowance to grieve albeit in different ways. The lover feels pain in a way the friend never will but that doesn't make it less important to either person. The child might feel ripped apart by the death of a parent while the spouse must figure out a way to keep going.

Life without death is impossible; death without life is the same.

Whatever it is that you're feeling has been felt before by someone else; nothing about death happens for the first time however it is the first time you've experienced it. You don't have to go through it alone.

I no longer fear of death because I've been walking alongside it for as long as I can remember. It's been my shadow on this journey, and I've finally gotten to a place where I understand that death is a gateway to a new life.

Sounds weird, right? But death is precisely that; the beginning of your life without that person being physically in it. It's a new beginning even though it feels like every door slams in your face and you're trapped, alone, in a hell created by the ending of their life.

Knowing this doesn't mean death and I are pals or that I don't grieve when someone passes away but I know it's not the end of anything. The physical death, to someone who has been slapped in the face for the first time by its cold ass hand, is like a defibrillator to the soul, bringing it back to life while a loved one transition into another. Sometimes it works, and sometimes it takes more than one loss to wake the fuck up. For me, it took the loss of seven people I loved before I understood why death surrounded me. When I look back over my life and count the number of times someone has died who I've known, the number is into the 30s. On average, that's about one death for every 14 months I've been alive. I wasn't as emotionally connected to them as I was to the people whose stories I share in this book. That's not to say their deaths (or lives) didn't matter; it simply means I wasn't jolted into another ascension on this journey by crossing paths with them. However, I honour them just the same.

Darkness has been the greatest gift I've received because it made the light I now live with, so much brighter.

A hundred candles

can flicker

and burn out,

but you only notice the darkness

when the light around you,

fades away

Hey Karen,

I've been thinking about why Travis was in my life, and a part of it was to connect me to you. Now before you get all weepy, know this: You became such a good friend but let's be honest here, I just wanted to stay in Travis' life HA! KIDDING!! If it weren't for you, I don't know if Trav and I would have stayed connected. You kept us together, and I came to love you as much as I loved him.

Some people leave your life, and you could care less whether you reconnect but then there are friends you see again, and it's like no time had passed. I hate that our time together was so short but I'm grateful for the memories we made together. You still have a lot of life to live so make sure you embrace every moment, every tear, every laugh, and all the love because we both know he wouldn't want it any other way.

I'm here if you need me.

Love,

t.

A true champion: Joe's story

January 7, 2015

I met my dear husband our marriage was something I was proud because we waited to find "true love." Yes, it does still exist, and my hopeless romantic husband is one of them.

We were married in Oct 2005 and two years later had our first daughter, Giorgia and second daughter Lucia a year after. Joe has always prided himself on being a family man, and even though circumstances have hindered his capabilities, he is our true hero.

Battling brain cancer (Glioblastoma Multiform Grade 4 cancer) has not only been the challenge of his life (and he thought it was being married to me, ha ha), it has shown us compassion, love, and humanity. It has taught us that taking days and moments for granted isn't an option and even though we have had LOTS of terrible days, Joe always finds a reason to be grateful.

On December 13, 2011, the diagnosis came back, and before Joe could start treatment, we found ourselves back in ER on January 1, 2012, to find out the brain tumour had grown in the past two weeks. The diagnosis meant he most likely would not make it to treatment. Joe's brain tumour was inoperable! News that my husband might die within the month was more than my young family could bear. Even with the odds against him, Joe not only made it through 6 weeks of gruelling in-patient treatment at the Cross Cancer Institute, but he also continues his battle, now 33 months and counting, which is 24 months more than the average patient's life expectancy with an inoperable GBM tumour.

He has fought long and hard and kept getting up after each time they said, "You have a second tumour," or "You have a third tumour." He made it through doctors telling him, "Your second and third tumours have grown together and are quite large," and, "Your tumours are still growing we have run out of options." He took every possible chemo they offered to him. He never said, "No I'm done." He has always had hope.

My girls had gotten to know their Daddy. Our youngest was only two years old the first time the diagnosis came in. We've had time to create loving, lasting and impressionable memories for the girls and me.

Although our future seems dismal, my husband continues to soar on, and for that, I feel Joe is a Champion! Brain cancer will take his life one day, but it will not take his integrity and passion for his family. He *has inspired and blessed so many people.*

You'd think they inspired him with ongoing support, but so many friends, family, and colleagues have thanked Joe for giving them hope and reason to believe.

Thank you for allowing Joe to be part of this lovely event and experience. It's a privilege to have him as my husband.

Corinna Spaziani

I've only had to do this once since I launched the FIERCE awards and it fucking sucks.

Joe Spaziani, a diamond recipient in our 2014 Champion category, had been battling a brain tumour for 31 months when his wife, Corinna, nominated him for a FIERCE award. Today, less than three months after we celebrated his accomplishments, contributions and the differences he made in the lives of those he touched, and 37 months after his diagnosis, he passed away.

I had the chance to hug Joe a couple of times when I met him at the Diamond Celebration where all of the recipients gathered to meet on September 27, 2014. I could tell by his demeanor that he was a gentle soul with a beautiful heart. He exuded warmth and love, but he was definitely a fighter. When I saw Joe a month later at the FIERCE awards, I hugged him again after he received his Diamond and he smiled down at me (I swear he must have been 8 feet tall) and told me how much the event meant to him. I replied that I was grateful that he was a part of our 5th and final event and that he was deserving of the recognition for all that he had done.

My heart is heavy with sadness tonight. I hate writing these things. It only reminds me that it's crucial to celebrate life while we are here and that the people you love deserve to be told as often as possible because you never know if you'll get another chance.

The world lost a beautiful soul today, but his life will not be forgotten.

7

Death doesn't fuck around

Hey Tamara,

In the summer of 2016, I joined an incredibly talented team of people, working for our boss, Ruth, and side-by-side with you. I didn't know the challenges she was facing with her publishing company, none of us did until later that year and well into 2017.

We had a steadfast loyalty to Ruth and an unwavering trust in her ability to find a way out of the mess.

It turns out that watching a company crumble is only part of the story, not the worst part, though. The seldom talked about part of watching a person you love unravel in front of you and being helpless to stop it is the worst part. Ruth was someone we loved and respected. She was someone who challenged you, frustrated you, infuriated you but still made you better at your job. And she was someone we couldn't help when she needed us the most.

You and I dealt with the uncertainty of the situation different and the same. I could never quite tell if you loved or hated her, but now I'm pretty sure it was both You loved her for making you better and hated her continually pushing you to be better, but mostly you were incredibly proud to have Ruth as a friend rather than a boss. As things got worse at work for everyone, you became more frustrated about the situation. Most of the time, you and I joked about being the band on the deck of the Titanic playing as it sunk, arguing about *which instrument we each had. Other times, we were each other's sounding board on how to best keep everyone else motivated. And sometimes it was so effing sad we could barely make eye contact. You made my days tolerable during that time.*

For most of us, it finally became too painful to watch the business fall apart, day by day, and to watch her slowly break down, in the same way. So, we left the company for our survival. For the others who stayed, they could only avert their eyes and continue to believe she would find a way to fix everything.

It's a long fall off a pedestal when imploding into rubble is the only outcome.

But here's what I learned; to help someone who was as strong as Ruth was, she had to be willing to admit she needed help. She needed to become vulnerable and accept help. For her to take her own life, means she wasn't able to accept that.

She didn't allow me in very far, but even if she had, I'm not sure I would have been able to see her as vulnerable or in need of my help. I think I would have told her, in complete sincerity, and the absolute belief in her, "It will be okay, you'll find a way to do this." I think I DID tell her that even though I knew how impossible the situation was. And that was probably the worst thing anyone could have said to her. I wonder how many people tried to uplift her spirits by saying that? I know she would never have shared the entire story, but she trusted parts of it to some of us. No one listened or heard the pedestal crack and break.

Maybe, just maybe, you and I have learned enough to be able to listen differently and listen to the words someone doesn't say.

I know Ruth joins us every time we get together. She will always be at the table with us, laughing and sharing memories.

Love,
Sue

"Hey, what's up?"

"She committed suicide."

"What? What did you say?"

Death doesn't fuck around.

There are no profound last goodbyes or a final conversation that I can carry with me when it comes to the death of my mentor, friend, and two-time former boss. The truth is, I didn't think I would be sitting there grieving over the abrupt ending to her life only 12 days after Travis' funeral.

Her death was all over the news because of who she was. The morning after I got that phone call, I sat at my desk, trying not to lose my fucking mind and desperately trying to make sense of it all. How could two of the most important people in my life die so suddenly from entirely different causes? I raced through my conversations with her, hopelessly searching for something, anything, she might have said to me that should have made me see what she had planned.

Nothing was there.

If I looked hard enough, maybe I could have seen it coming, but I knew that nothing I said or anyone could have said would have changed her mind.

I wasn't even close to being over the sudden loss of Travis, but with her death, I had to set aside that grief and let the pain of losing her consume me. I felt momentarily paralyzed. I closed my eyes and quietly let the tears flow because I knew enough to give into what I was feeling.

"What the fuck am I supposed to learn from this?" I thought, holding my head in my hands and taking slow, deep breaths while my thumbs alternately rubbed my temples. The building across the street had cast a shadow through my window, and I sat there, wondering what I could have done differently, how her husband was coping with her death and asking myself why she would have done that to him. Death was everywhere, and there was no escaping it.

I sat there, my hands covering my face, asking myself why death enjoyed taking people from my life when the sun hit the windows of the building across from me. Light reflected over my face, warming my entire being. I looked up, almost blinded by the brightness, and felt a calming sense of peace wash over me. I felt her presence in the sun as if to remind me that darkness doesn't last forever.

As social media and local news outlets exploded in shock, I couldn't hide from her death. Everywhere I looked, someone was posting condolences at the sudden loss of such an influential woman. I, however, was barely stumbling out of the fog of losing Travis the same day I started a new job which was mere weeks after leaving my position with Ruth's company. It was the second time in my career that I had worked for her and quitting wasn't as easy as it should have been. In my entire life, there have been a handful of people who I ever gave a shit about what they thought of me, and Ruth was at the top of that list. The idea of letting her down or disappointing her weighed heavily on my heart, but Sue was right. I had no choice when it came to leaving the company. Another opportunity presented itself, and I would have been stupid to turn it down.

I sat in my office, blindsided in shock from both deaths, trying to understand what was happening around me.

Of all the losses I had lived through, this time, death won. Nothing I'd experienced in my life - not the deaths leading up to hers, and not the violence and pain I'd experienced in my childhood - prepared me for what I was about to learn.

I felt my soul crack in places it hadn't broken before, and I knew the ending of her life would be the beginning of something but had no idea what that was. Death has a ripple effect, and everyone who was touched by Ruth's life mourned her differently. My relationship with her was mine to grieve, but I wasn't oblivious to the pain other people were feeling. If she had died from cancer or been hit by a bus, the grief would have been the same however the fact that she chose to end her life amplified the shock because no one expected such a strong, influential woman to go out that way. From the outside, people saw her as a poised leader, inspirational mentor, compassionate philanthropist and successful entrepreneur which is why the shock of her suicide blindsided so many people.

In the 17 years I had known her, she was the only woman I had looked to as a maternal figure after being without one for most of my life. Then just like that, she was gone.

Death was everywhere, and I grasped at every lesson

I had learned from every other loss I had experienced to get through this moment in my life.

- Realize it's happened and nothing you do can change it
- Feel all the emotions
- Cry
- Vent
- Be angry
- Embrace sadness
- Remember that death isn't the end
- You can still talk to her
- Watch for the signs and messages because they will be there
- Process it
- Fall back into the pain if it hasn't healed
- Look at the stars and know there is a reason for all of this
- Learn the lesson from her life and death

All of this happened about a month before I was part of a book launch of a compilation of stories from women around the world called *Modern Heroine Soul Stories*. I was proud to be a part of that book, but with everything going on, I wasn't able to entirely focus on the launch, so I sent an email to Molly, the woman behind *Modern Heroine*. We had kept in touch over the years through social media and but I hadn't spoken to her much since my mom passed away until she reached out and asked me to be a part of the book she was producing. I was grateful that she even thought of me as someone who had something of value to add to her book. I gladly shared a chapter of my story but now was unable to find the energy to focus on the launch.

June 15, 2017, 9:22 am Gmail

Hey Molly,

My mentor died two days ago. Actually, she committed suicide. Between her death and Travis' death a couple of weeks ago, starting this new job and not knowing what bullshit reality TV script my life will be next week, my head is spinning. I don't know how much help I'm going to be for you to promote this book right now. I can repost on FB/Instagram, but beyond that, I can barely keep my head above water. I'm doing everything I can to focus on work so that I don't get lost in my head. Honestly, I feel like I'm in robot-mode. It's probably a good time to write, ha. I don't know. I guess I'll go through the motions until I come out of this haze.

I'm probably going to be quiet online for a bit. You know where to find me if you need me.

Love,

t.

In her beautifully gracious way, Molly's response was to help me understand why death shadowed my life.

June 15, 2017, 11:22 am Gmail

Oh wow...what a shock... I am so sorry. :(That is heartbreaking especially on the heels of Travis' passing, too.

I just got this crazy immediate download for you... it's in the attached recording. I hope it brings just a little bit of comfort as you move through this time.

Reposting about the book anywhere is great when you feel like it but I completely understand and respect where you're at and what you're feeling. No expectations.

Take really good care of yourself and keep me posted. I'll reach out if anything comes up.

Love,

Molly

I couldn't bring myself to play the recording she had sent because my emotions were raw and I was doing everything possible to contain the chaos inside my heart. I moved through the next few days in a blur, operating on autopilot and refusing to allow the sadness to overwhelm me.

I tapped into every tool I'd gathered up to that point:

➢ Meditation

➢ Leaning on guidance from the angels

➢ Feeling every fucking emotion I had the moment I had it regardless of how much pain it caused

➢ Reminding myself that death wasn't their real end, only their physical journey in this lifetime

➢ Rising above the grief and helping others where I could

Confusion and anger from Ruth's choice to end her life coursed through my veins and settled in like an old friend. I sat with my grief, and for the first time in my life, began to wonder why death surrounded me. I had never asked myself that question before but with two losses, weeks of each other, of two people I loved, deeply and differently, it made me wonder why?

A few weeks passed, and I remembered the email that Molly had sent. I opened the message and downloaded the recording to my phone, unsure if I was ready to hear what she had to tell me but knowing that if I ignored it for too long, I'd risk reopening the grief wound later on. Taking a deep breath, I hit play.

"Hey Tamara, thank you for letting me know what's going on and, wow, it's understandably a tough time with these two passings," she began, taking a deep sigh as if she could feel my pain. "I'm so sorry because obviously it's tough enough to deal with your brother's death and then for your mentor's suicide. I mean there's so much wrapped up in suicide." I paused the recording, biting my lip to stop myself from crying because I could hear the sadness I felt in Molly's voice.

"I just felt this inclination to share with you a little bit of what's happening in your birth chart because you have a few big oppositions and oppositions are the feeling of something that's out of our control," she continued, going back into healer mode.

"One of the things that can show up in an astrology chart is powerful themes of what the soul is learning in this lifetime, and you have such powerful Scorpio energy.

It's in multiple places in your chart. You are much deeper on the inside, and you process more things than most people are aware of and there are big life transformations with relationships. Each one of these relationships is a part of you, and it shapes you, and it's almost like a part of you leaves when they die.

"You've had a lot of death around you and people passing in your life. It's an ongoing theme. It can feel like there's this sense of you leaving when they go. It's really important for you to be aware of how it all affects your self-worth and your connection with spirit and trusting that you're on this path for a reason. It's all those things that we 'know,' but our human selves have to go through it and experience it, intensely and deeply and emotionally.

"The thing that came to me right away is that because you have such strong, powerful Scorpio energy, you also have a powerful spiritual karmic energy. So I feel like one of your soul missions is actually," she paused again as the emotions rushed to the surface, fighting back the tears. "You, as a soul said, 'I'm going to know this person so I can help them transition to the next lifetime. I'm going to be someone who holds a space for them, who holds an energy for them."

That was it. The tears flowed, and I could no longer stop them as I listened to Molly's message.

"I feel like it's a karmic thing where other people saved your life in other lifetimes, and you are balancing the energy and paying them back being their support by helping them energetically transition. So, it can feel like you magnetize people who are about to die. You've been through this so many times in your life, and you think, 'What's the deal?' But at a soul level, I feel that this is intentional because I feel like you're at the place now where you've learned so much, spiritually, and you've grown so much. And you know this. You know your connection with angels and spirit guides. They give you more reassurance and greater support which in turn allows you to be this human vessel, a support for other people, energetically at least.

"I remember hearing a story, like 15 or 20 years ago, of a person who always found himself driving past car wrecks. It would be on his commute to work or with his family, and there would be a backup of traffic, and it was like, 'Oh my gosh, is there another car accident?' He was always around when there was a fatality in these car wrecks. Through a psychic reading, he came to understand that was one of his soul's commitments was to be there energetically to help that person transition," she fought back the tears again, but her voice broke as she struggled to finish the message. "He was there to let them know it's OK to go and I feel like that's one of your gifts. You are the one who can tell somebody, energetically, spiritually in whatever form that it's OK to go. It's OK. And you can feel differently as your human self, but I feel like the highest you knows that you're going to be the helping hand that helps them leave this earthly experience so that their soul can keep going forward. They can feel at peace or feel greater peace about leaving.

"It's kind of like you're a hospice nurse or that sense of the in-between person, energetically. Now, you still will feel the impact of their death, and you will feel it deeply, but that's because you can go there, emotionally, and you can be in that partnership with them of understanding that, for whatever reasons, their time here was just done. And it takes more spiritual growth to let that go.

It was like a light switch the way her emotions left her body once she got that message out because she eased back into the healer messenger that she is.

"You have your moon in Libra, conjunct Pluto in the 12th house and it's such powerful energy for you in regards to the spiritual understandings because with the 12th house planets, you can feel like an ongoing victim. Like, 'Oh my God, why does this always happen to me?' The self-pity comes up, the self-blame, the need to escape through alcohol or drugs or thinking, 'I need to go and do something that takes me out of this reality because I can't deal with everything that is so messed up.' But as you spiritually evolve and grow you start to rise above that feeling of self-pity or self-blame or victimness where it's like, 'Why does this always happen to me?' and you begin to see it as part of your spiritual path. Everything transitions, everything changes form, everything changes energy, and it allows you to be more in touch with your angels and guides because you're rising into that greater place of a spiritual perspective.

"There is still very much the human emotions when you experience grief, but there's so much wisdom in it. But I feel so strongly that you have elevated your energy to the point where this information, this understanding of yourself, resonates and you realize that, ugh, I'm listening for the words," she said. "It's like you realize that you are a conduit, a death conduit. Being a conduit from this lifetime into other lifetimes is letting that person go, and you could feel that they come and speak with you through dreams or meditation or you feel their energy, and they're talking to you, and you can be that partner for them, the one who understands.

The grief returned to her voice, and she fought to get the words out.

"I feel like it's imperative to allow yourself to own this as part of your soul gifts.

"I'm really sorry. It's big stuff, but you're strong, and you've been through things. You'll always be OK. Losing two people you loved within weeks of each other still hurts the heart but it's something you will move through.

"The other thing that's happening in your chart is that the Pluto opposition is occurring with your Saturn in your Cancer, so it brings up childhood by triggering how you felt as a child, but it's helping you to see that you're now the adult version of yourself. The Pluto at 18 degrees of Capricorn is making a supportive sextile to your Sun and Venus in Scorpio, so that tells me that you are going to have some good things that come out of this time. I feel it as something as more related to speaking, writing and sharing your different losses. And I'm hearing that the book title could be something like Seven Deaths or something related to seven. I don't know if seven is the number of people you've lost or if seven has a meaning for you but it keeps coming up. Maybe it's a short book, and it talks about the different people you've had to say goodbye to and what each of those people meant to you or what you've learned. Every transition was different, every person was different, and you were different for each person's transition.

"Take good care of yourself and, yes, write if that helps process it all. Also, know that you're starting a new 12-year cycle. Jupiter is at 13 degrees in your first house beginning a new relationship cycle, which means new people are coming into your life. That includes new relationships, new partnerships, so that's going to be some good, fresh energy.

"I'm just sorry, Tamara. I'm sorry that you are going through this to get to the next phase of your life. I honour and respect where you're at right now, and I hope that this recording sheds some light or offers some comfort on what you're experiencing.

"You know where I am if you need me. Take really good care."

***

A few weeks later, I had a dream. I was across the

street from the office where I worked with Ruth, looking at the building when I saw someone go in through the doors. That didn't make sense because the space had been empty since we moved to another building before her death.

I went over and walked in, looking around, and yelled, "Hello? Who's here?"

No one answered, so I walked up the stairs to the main desk only to see a woman come out of Ruth's office.

"Who are you?" I demanded. "You can't be in Ruth's office!"

"It's time to move forward," she said with a concerned but gentle smile on her face.

I looked around and saw that the once dark, brick walls were now bright white. Everything was lit up, and I suddenly became aware of what was happening. Ruth came out of her office and laughed at my reaction.

"It's time to move forward, Tamara," she said, smiling at me, almost amused at the look on my face. Although I knew she had come to say goodbye, I was skeptical of her acceptance of what was going on. In life, my comments about spirituality and the universe were met with nods of disbelief, and she humoured my challenges to her reluctance to believe there was more to death than the end of your body.

"Are you sure?" I asked, torn between not wanting this to be our last conversation and knowing she needed to go.

The look of happiness on her face was the only response I needed, but she laughed at me anyway.

I smiled at her and nodded, saying "OK, I know."

She followed me out of the building, and as the door closed behind us, I looked back at her and smiled. She returned the emotion, and we both went our separate ways.

The Lessons:

Death is about the people who are left behind to mourn. No one knows for sure what happens when someone dies; everyone has their belief system that they cling to in hopes of understanding why they have been left to suffer.

By this point, I had already experienced enough conversations with spirits of the people I loved to know they weren't dreams, and I wasn't crazy. I was open to the messages they had for me, and looked forward to seeing them after they'd passed.

Whether you lose someone suddenly or watch them die over any length of time, the result is the same; you are left to live. I hate to break it to you, but you're going to die, too. However, you can't live in fear of death because that's not living, but you can't find another way out of this life, either.

We search for answers after we experience loss:

Why?

Will I ever see them again?

How do I move forward?

The answers we seek are within us, and it takes soul searching to find them. Some people are more pragmatic than others and understand they can't control death, but they can control how they move forward. Other people need to find those answers before they can move on and there's no right or wrong way for getting through it. Part of your journey is accepting loss and understanding that people will come and go from your life whether it's through heartbreak or death.

Death can wake you up to change your behaviour and your life, but transformation only happens when you are ready.

Some questions you might ask yourself are:

How do I want to live the next chapter of my life?

Where do I need to improve or change?

Do I need to carry them with me or should I let that part of me die with them?

Other questions might follow:

Would they forgive me for moving forward? *(Hell yes, they would want you to move forward! Love isn't about holding someone back, and spirits don't operate from a place of ego like humans do. They operate from love because they are love)*

What if I'm never ready to let them go? *(You will be, on your own time and your terms.)*

Will I forget them? *(You don't forget people you love even when they pass away. You end up honouring them by living and keeping their memory in your heart)*

In Sue's letter, she expressed the idea that maybe both of us learned to read the signs of someone who was going through a traumatic situation. In my experience, anyone who has committed suicide has been determined to follow through with it. Nothing I could have said or done would have stopped them. There is guilt associated with suicide; you wonder what you did or didn't do, question why you didn't see the signs until after or beat yourself up because you ignored the cries for help. You're already going through enough turmoil so adding guilt to the mix isn't going to help. Grief is like being under a thousand blankets, each one carrying a different emotion. The weight can suffocate you, so there's no benefit to your sanity or wellness by allowing guilt to be the most onerous burden of them all.

Keep the people you love alive in your heart by talking about them and remembering the good and bad. No one is perfect, so there's no point in putting anyone on a pedestal after their death. Laugh about the dumb things you did together and find comfort in the time that you had with them. No, you won't get any more time with them in this lifetime, so there's no point wishing they were here to make new memories. They'll stay with you in spirit and guide you as you move through this journey if you allow them to help you. To do that, you have to ask for their help.

If you're expecting a visit from them in a dream and they don't appear, it's not because they don't want to but usually because you are dealing with enough grief and they are unable to connect with you. If you want them to visit, you have to be open, but it's not as easy as it sounds. Dream visitations can shake you to the core because the pain of not being able to hug them or see them when you wake up is sometimes more emotional than finding out about their death. These dreams are a gateway to healing, but they're not the only way you can connect with a loved one.

How else can you talk to someone who has passed?

Sit in silence and listen.

Loved ones often come through when we're quiet and

ready to hear them. They compete with the noise around you so turn off the phone, close your eyes and breathe. Think of a memory and hold onto that moment. Allow the conversation to flow. Don't ask questions; sit and let the words come through. When we're awake, we overthink and tune out messages that we are seeking. That is why spirits come to us in dreams or when we're meditating.

Watch for the signs

Message from the dead will often come through when you least expect it. Recently (in the middle of writing this book), I was concerned about work and finances one day, so I asked my angels for a clear sign that everything would be OK. That afternoon, I was taking the bus and sat across from a woman who promptly struck up a conversation. I looked at my phone hoping she would take the hint but she continued to ask questions. I looked up and glanced at her as she smiled. I listened as she prattled on about her day and she began to tell me about her life.

She was in her late 40s with long, auburn hair and a smile that lit up her face. She captured my complete attention when she said, "You should go to bingo! I bet you'd win. Everything will be OK for you."

In my head, I was all, "What the fuuuuuuck? Who is this woman?!" before realizing she reminded me of my mom! Everything from her voice to her smile to her mention of bingo (my mom loved bingo but seriously, does anyone play that anymore?). I was floored until I realized she was the answer to the questions I had asked my angels. This woman said she often told people things they needed to hear.

Ask them to contact you

If you want them to talk to you, you must tell them to reach out. Sometimes you won't hear them because they're not getting through the veil between the human life and the afterlife so ask them to speak up. Tell them to be clear and to do what they need to do to get your attention. If you ask, don't be surprised when they reach out. If you shut them down or refuse to listen, they will pull back or find another way to contact you.

After my grandfather passed away, he came to me in a dream even though I wasn't quite asleep. He walked into my bedroom, looking like he did when he was in his 40s, and said, "Tamara, get up! I have to show you something!"

I refused and said, "Nope, not doing this! Your funeral is in a couple of days. I won't do this." He grabbed my hand and yanked me out of the sleeping position, and I woke up, looking around and feeling the pressure of his thumb in the palm of my hand. The thing is, he had lost his thumb in a workplace accident before I was born. I crawled under the covers and sobbed myself back to sleep.

The next morning, I woke up and my three-year-old daughter came out of her room and crawled into my lap. "Great gramma and great grampa we here last night," she said. I looked at her and asked what she meant. She repeated herself, slowly, as though she was trying to be patient with my stupidity.

"I don't understand," I said. She told me great grampa went to her room and brought her to the kitchen where great gramma was waiting. "They said they were together forever and that they were so proud of you, mama. They said I was just like you." Her little face beamed with pride because she knew something I didn't. She ran off to her room and came back with a bowl and shoved it at me. "They got me grapes, mama!" An empty grape stem was in the bowl, and I burst into tears. I was unwilling to listen to my grandfather's request so he went to my daughter to give me the message and I missed the opportunity to see my grandmother again.

When Travis passed away, I waited patiently for him to come and say goodbye. When he did, he brought the bottle of whiskey I'd given him for his birthday and poured a shot for both of us. He sat across from me, raised his glass and smiled that shit-eatin' grin of his before downing the shot. I woke up smiling, grateful to see his face one last time.

The past is history
and cannot be rewritten;
the future
is where randomness exists.

Every step taken,
everything experienced,
and every choice
brings you to this moment
of perceived randomness.
From here, you have free will;
a decision which leads
to the next phase
of this choose-your-own adventure.

Conversation with Kelly

Oct. 12, 2017

It's 3 a.m., and I can't sleep. Death has been breathing down my neck and his breath reeks of the devil's ass, if I believed in the devil, that is. My guess is that the devil's ass would smell like a hot and putrid zombie-apocalypse after a rainstorm. Anyway, I can't sleep because death has another message for me and even though I'm not sure at this moment what it is, if I don't start writing, I might sleep forever this time.

There have been chunks of my life where I've been dormant and unwilling to acknowledge who I had become despite being shaken by death as if violently guiding me to yet another ascension, another level of who I am supposed to be. I'd snap out of the slumber then close my eyes and refuse to see myself for who I was despite the fact that I could feel myself changing.

The initial sting of death hurts the most, more than any other pain you could ever feel in your life. Losing someone is supposed to hurt; it means you loved someone enough to have your heart shatter into a million pieces and feel like it will never repair itself. That's the funny thing about the heart, though. It breaks and mends a thousand times stronger than you ever imagined with time, acceptance and reflection of what that person meant to you while they were here.

I don't know why it took me this long to come out of the fog and accept that death has been part of my soul purpose. I guess no one wants to think about death or experience it or even talk about it, but I can't ignore or escape it so I might as well try to share what I've learned.

Like I said earlier, thoughts of death have me awake at 3 a.m. for no other reason than to write this part of the book.

Except now I know why. I'm relatively active on Twitter (you can connect with me @YouAreFIERCE) and this morning, one of my long-time followers and friend, who recently lost her husband, started chatting with me.

I am Tamara @YouAreFIERCE
1:08 am 12 Oct 2017
Insomnia sucks. The minute I think I'm falling asleep, all the things pop into my head.

Kelly Buckley @Kelly_A_Bee 44m
Right?!?!?!? Ugh! #wideawake

I am Tamara @YouAreFIERCE 30 m
Same since 11:30pm. I'm going to write this out of my system.
Book 3 is has a deadline. How are you?

Kelly Buckley @Kelly_A_Bee 25m
I'm alright…More good days than bad. Grateful for my fam and
friends

I am Tamara @YouAreFIERCE 22m
The bad days are reminders that you're still alive. The pain is
something you carry with you forever but it numbs after a while.

Kelly Buckley @Kelly_A-Bee 17m
Thanks for that. I know you're carrying your share of pain too… You
had a hard summer.

I am Tamara @YouAreFIERCE 15m
I'm turning that pain into Book 3. Couldn't figure out why I've been
surrounded by death my whole life. Blessing in disguise?

Kelly Buckley @Kelly_A-Bee 11m
Maybe… I'm still too raw to see the blessing…One day perhaps.
Until then, the only way forward is through – and trying to be open.

I am Tamara @YouAreFIERCE 9m
Oh no, I meant for me, it was a blessing in disguise. I figured some
shit out bc of what I experienced. I would never suggest that for
you.

Kelly Buckley @Kelly_A-Bee 11m
Ahhh…well, I can say you definitely learn things about yourself.
Grief is very disorienting. And constantly changing.

After that tweet, we switched to Direct Messages.

> This might seem like an odd request, but can I use this thread as part of the chapter I'm writing? I'll be OK if you say no.

Oh – that's unexpected! But for sure – I don't mind at all.

> I woke up to write but I wasn't sure why. Now I know. It's 3 a.m., and I can't sleep. Death has been breathing down my neck and his breath reeks of the devil's ass, if I believed in the devil, that is. My guess is that the devil's ass would smell like a hot and putrid zombie-apocalypse after a rainstorm. Anyway, I can't sleep because death has another message for me and even though I'm not sure at this moment what it is, if I don't start writing, I might sleep forever this time.

Wow. Oh my.

> Yeh, I think I woke up for a reason. Thanks for letting me share the thread in the book!

Well – I guess you and I were meant to have this conversation tonight… I couldn't fall asleep tonight. Laid in bed from 10pm until almost 3am. Yesterday would have been my 8th wedding anniversary and P has been on my mind. I got up to write him a letter… sometimes I find that if I write him an email and talk to him like he's here, it settles my mind. I cry, release emotion, and then I can fall asleep. Tonight, I was still restless. And then our conversation *smile emoji*

Whoa, what the hell!! I haven't woken up like this to write in a long time but something made me get online and start writing. So I just started typing whatever came to mind. I channel write a lot so I just let the words flow. This was definitely guided by a higher power. Maybe there's an angel message I can give you if you want? I do angel card readings.

I would love that…

Ok one sec

I pulled three cards for Kelly, two from *Messages from Angels Oracle Cards* and one from the *Ascended Masters Deck*, both created by Doreen Virtue. The first card was Mystique: Keep charging ahead, and don't take no for an answer. Expect miraculous solutions to appear."

The second card was Isaiah: It's a good time to give birth to new ideas and situations in your life. I am watching over you, guiding you, and protecting you during these changes.

The final card was the Hindu Goddess, Paravati: Positive Change.

The cards tell an interesting story so I don't know what's going on with you personally but the angels are telling me you are going through a change, new beginning of sorts. You're protected with this change so if you're concerned about it, don't be. Be confident and expect the best outcome for your greatest and highest good. Paravati is the Goddess of Mountains so maybe you are being guided to retreat to the mountains for time to yourself or matbe the mountains represent a place you enjoyed with your husband? Not sure but mountains are important here.

Also you need to say no to people. That comes up strongly in these cards.

We were married in the mountains. Golden. Always as special place for us.

OK this is weird... I'm going to send you a picture.

Paravati is the Hindu goddess of mountains, marriage, and households. Legend says that Shiva the Hindu god was grief stricken following the death of his first love, Sati, so he retreated to a mountain cave. When Paravati was born in the mountains, Shiva fell in love with her devotion to helping the planet. They became united in love and had a son, Ganesh. Call upon Paravati for solace and solutions to any seeming problem, especially if you're meditating in the mountains.

Ascended Masters Oracle Cards Guide Book
by Doreen Virtue

I continued the conversation:

> Lord Ganesh is a cool God to know. He often guides me so I'm not surprised to see was with me for this message. This card is important for you. Anyway, I hope this brings you some comfort and makes sense.

Ummm...shivers...This gives me a lot of peace, Tamara. I've spent a lot of time the past few months thinking about how to go on, start living again and finding joy. I am hopeful that I am on the right path.

> You are!! Trust in that. The angels always give me the right messages to share and I'm glad you were open to it.

Much love to you.

Spiral up

She had reached this ascension
through unearthing past traumas,
and doing the dirty work to forgive.

She let go
when all I could do was cling

She returned to chapters I had written,
wrapping her arms
around past versions of who I was,
thanking them for not giving up

and enduring endless pain.

It took time

days
weeks
months
and years

so many years

but she released them all

one by one

and slowly cemented
a kintsugi masterpiece
together with love

stronger
beautiful
energetically potent

The light beamed
through her scars

she had survived

And now that she completed her ascension
I said goodbye

reluctantly

unwilling to believe
the demons were not restlessly waiting
for my moment of weakness
to resurrect

and destroy
everything I had become

She smiled gently
offering a warm embrace

Tamara Plant

infusing my soul with light

assurance
that the demons were at peace

and so was I

she turned to ash

and I stood up
covered in remains

eyes closed

peaceful
for the first time in my life
finally understanding why

finally

finally

ashes incarnate

blessed with this journey

inspired to inspire

my life was
written in the stars

beautiful scars

I finally understood why

and knew then

I am love.

It took being

fucked up
messed up
shattered

almost giving up

time
after time
after time
after time

to get here

I keep spiraling upwards
on this everlasting ascension

with gratitude
for the souls
who had battled before me

and the promise to continue their fight.

Tamara Plant

202

Epilogue

When Molly said I was a conduit of death, I thought that was weird but she says a lot of things to me that I think are weird at the time until I understand what she was trying to say. Great, I thought, everyone who comes into my life is doomed! DOOMED!! No wonder I don't maintain long-term relationships, I thought. They all end up dead or scared they're going to end up dead when they find out how many people I know have died. Fuck. Makes a lot of sense now, I told myself.

And then I became hyper aware of how people, random strangers, would tell me the most intimate details of their lives for no apparent reason. I could be at a grocery store or on the bus and someone would strike up a conversation, spilling their deepest secrets. I've come to see this as a fragile gift; the ability to connect with someone who needs support or someone to listen to them is a blessing and curse because it drains my energy if I let it. Most times, I listen without interrupting and sometimes I see them as messengers who are there to answer questions I've been asking.

Death is their end, but it isn't ours.

If I've learned anything about death, it's that the people who are left to grieve are the ones who must also remember to live. Life must go on, and we must work through the heartache that is a part of the healing process.

I was a couple of months into writing this book when Archangel Gabriel whispered, "Conversations with..." and left me hanging to figure out what she meant. After sitting with that little nugget, the only word that kept popping into my head was, "Soulmates."

"That doesn't even make sense," I grumbled. "This book is about death, not soulmates."

"Isn't it, though?" she replied. I could see she was patiently leading me to the answer, smirking and somewhat amused with my response.

"Is it? How are death and soulmates connected? Haven't I learned enough fucking lessons in this lifetime? What the shit did I do in a past life to have to go through this?" I asked out loud.

By this point, I knew there was a reason and a lesson in everything and that I had to dig deep to figure out what that lesson was. Unlike my mom's death, forgiveness wasn't something I needed to learn. There had to be another reason, but I had no idea what the fuck death was trying to teach me this time.

One thing I knew for sure was that I changed every time death took someone away from me and was somehow a better person because of the people I'd lost. I looked at life differently and peeled away the layers of pain to reveal a light I never realized was there. I took a deep breath and looked at all the pieces of the puzzle from a more spiritual place, examining the lives that had passed through mine and wondering how it all fit together.

The only thread that connected everyone I had lost was love. And the only thread that connected love to death was soulmates. You can't have one without the other. I knew then that for this book to work, the messages had to come from soulmates, people who had seen me transform and go through various ascensions through the deaths I'd experienced. That's when I reached out to Karen, Karissa, Teresa, Sue, Sheena and Bernice. They had been a part of my life when I was levelling up; disintegrating to ash to become the version of myself they knew which eventually led me to this point in my life.

As for love, well, I had mixed feelings about love. I learned a long time ago to tell the people you love that YOU LOVE THEM because you might not get another chance. I love my friends, I love my life, I love my kids, I love this version of myself, and I love to see people happy. But why would love be the lesson I needed to learn?

Mushy, gross affections of love have never been my thing, but maybe there was something else to it. Perhaps the lesson wasn't about expressions of love. Perhaps it was about operating from the vibration of love and not in the *50 Shades of Grey* kinda way, I thought, smirking at my joke. No. No, no no! Couldn't be that, I told myself. Why the fuck would I need to operate from a place of love, I wondered?

Sexual innuendos? Sure.

Dirty jokes? Absolutely!

Saying, "I love you," to the people you love? Without a doubt.

But to operate from a core of love that tied everything from forgiveness, non-judgement, peace, tranquility, softness and purity? The first two, sure. The rest, fuck no.

Fuck.

No!

I closed my eyes and asked my angels the question, "Why would I ever need to vibe (hah, I said vibe) from a place of love? I can't even ask this without making fun of it! I know, I KNOW, I have to be serious here but honest to fuck, it's tough! You guys know me! You know I'm not good at this love shit so WHY?! Why do I have to do it?"

"To live, you must love."

"What the actual fuck? What does that even mean?" I asked, perturbed by their response.

"In death, there is no pain, no endings, nothing but love. When you are love, you elevate those around you and live from a higher purpose regardless of what's going on in your world. Through love, there is no judgement, no anger, no grief and no endings. You are living on purpose, with intention. Yes, it can be difficult to see love when someone projects hate, but that's when you have to get clear and focus. Hatred isn't living. Anger is pain; you are love, and the light around you shines to illuminate the path for others. And you have so much light."

Ugh. UGH!! Those words flowed through me as I wrote them and as much as I wanted to throw up in my mouth from all the saccharine, tears came to my eyes instead.

Yeah, yeah. Love. Got it, I thought. "Totally on it," I said, rolling my eyes. "Can I still have wine? Because I feel like this might take a lot of wine to make it happen."

"You have free will, so it's your choice. Listen to your body and your heart."

Ugh. The thing about angels is they won't tell you what to do, what you should do or how you need to live your life; they merely offer guidance based on what will serve your highest good. Even though I'm sure my angels were cringing at that moment thinking, "Don't be a dumbass, you don't need wine to operate from a place of love," they didn't have to say it; I knew what they were thinking.

The angels were right, but I had to ask them this: "Is it OK to get mad and angry and not see love?"

"Yes," they said. "You are living a human experience and have human emotions. Of course, you will feel what you feel but always come back to love. If love is at your core, you will never be alone no matter how much death is around you. And death, you know, is never the end."

I just had a fucking epiphany. Love is forgiveness and forgiveness starts with love. A-fucking-HA moment. When you forgive the darkness in others, you are operating from the highest form of love.

But what does this have to do with death?

It's all connected. When someone you love, dies, you're bound together by energy that transcends lifetimes. **Love, death, and soulmates are united by more than the physical form; you came from the stars and will someday return, guided by fate and surrounded by light.**

Death is a wakeup call to live; live your life on purpose, embrace the good and the bad, learn from the people who come into your life and do it all with love. Not *The Notebook*, Kumbaya-around-a-campfire, perma-grin, yogi-on-a-mountaintop, crying-at-a-sunset kinda love, either. Don't get crazy here. I'm talking about the kind of love that allows you to see the good in people when all they show you is hate.

The kind of love that makes you stop and be present in the moment when chaos envelops you.

The kind of love that allows you to transform from where you were to where you are with no regrets or fucks left to give.

The kind of love that wakes you up in the morning with gratitude and happiness for no other reason than being alive.

The kind of love that allows you to rest when you need to or be the pillar for someone when they can't stand on their own.

Love is fucking awesome but it doesn't have to be

sappy or romantic or tender and adoring; it can be kind and goofy and instantaneous and ridiculous. Love is whatever you decide it should be not what I say it is or what anyone else tells you it is.

Love connects soulmates, and not even death can separate them.

The people who have come into my life, whether they have stayed or not, have helped me ascend into this version of myself through pain, happiness, anger and everything other lesson they've shared.

The before and after of who you are changes with each soulmate who passes through your life. You're more likely to find me singing along to Eminem and dropping F-bombs instead of sitting on a mountaintop, chanting mantras, but that doesn't mean anything when it comes to living with love. I'm not a Saint, and I'm not going to pretend that I spread joy and sparkles everywhere I go, but I love infinitely and understand why death has been tapping my shoulder all these years. In the time I have left on this earth, I'll continue to live from a place of love and forgiveness (even though I still don't like yucky, mushy sentimentality, and I still twitch when someone wallows in victim mentality). What can I say? I embrace who I am, perceived flaws and all. It takes more energy to hold onto the agony of loss than to embrace gratitude and love for the moments you are blessed with in this lifetime.

Everyone has a shadow side even the people we perceive as "perfect."

Everyone fucks up.

Everyone lies, and if they tell you they never have, they're lying.

Everyone has hated someone or something.

Everyone is capable of love.

Everyone is capable of forgiveness.

Everyone is a soul who is meant to be in someone else's life.

Everyone is made of light.

It's the beautiful darkness of who we are.

Focus on the light or dark, and that's where you'll vibe from (HA! I said vibe, again :)

I'm on this never-ending ascension and maybe one day, one lifetime from now, I'll get to that place of love the angel was talking about and vibrate there every moment of every day.

Until then, I've made peace with death and embraced the love that has connected me to soulmates, grateful for the time I have with them, and understanding they can't stay in this lifetime forever.

Enjoy the ride,

learn the lessons,

trust the universe,

and live the fuck outta this lifetime.

Love,

T.

About the author

Tamara Plant is an international award-winning author who shared her story of overcoming adversity in her first book, *Forgiveness and Other Stupid Things*. She is published in the #1 Amazon international best-seller *Modern Heroine Soul Stories* and has a story in a collection called *Standing Together* published by the Alberta Council of Women's Shelters.

She hangs out on social media under the username YouAreFIERCE based on the online community she built in 2009.

Coffee is her bitch, and she has been known to fist-bump Archangel Michael while listening to Eminem. Look up the definition of spiritual badass, and you'll see Tamara's picture.

Oh, and she once watched *The Outsiders* while tweeting with S.E. Hinton. It was as awesome as it sounds.

95026412R00120

Made in the USA
Columbia, SC
10 May 2018